How to Talk to Anybody About Anything

How to Talk to Anybody About Anything

*Breaking the Ice
With Everyone
From Accountants
to Zen Buddhists*

Leil Lowndes

A CITADEL PRESS BOOK
Published by Carol Publishing Group

A Citadel Press Book
Published by Carol Publishing Group
Citadel Press is a registered trademark of Carol Communications, Inc.
Editorial Offices: 600 Madison Avenue, New York, N.Y. 10022
Sales and Distribution Offices: 120 Enterprise Avenue, Secaucus, N.J. 07094
In Canada: Canadian Manda Group, P.O. Box 920, Station U, Toronto,
    Ontario M8Z 5P9
Queries regarding rights and permissions should be addressed to Carol
Publishing Group, 600 Madison Avenue, New York, N.Y. 10022

Carol Publishing Group books are available at special discounts for bulk purchases, for sales promotion, fund-raising, or educational purposes. Special editions can be created to specifications. For details, contact: Special Sales Department, Carol Publishing Group, 120 Enterprise Avenue, Secaucus, N.J. 07094

Manufactured in the United States of America
10 9 8 7 6 5 4 3 2 1

Library of Congress Cataloging-in-Publication Data

Lowndes, Leil.
    How to talk to anybody about anything : breaking the ice with everyone from accountants to Zen Buddhists / by Leil Lowndes.
        p.   cm.
    "A Citadel Press Book."
    ISBN 0-8065-1458-2
    1. Conversation.
BJ2121.L68   1993
302.3′46—dc20   93-11588
                                                        CIP

Directory

---

v

Acknowledgments

I want to thank the hundreds of people who gave me a visitor's pass with full linguistic privileges to their worlds, and who agreed to talk to me in *their* languages. Especially helpful were publications editors who deal daily with the issues and the words of their readers.

In each chapter there is a special thank you to people who were of greatest assistance. So my acknowledgment does not condemn them with their colleagues, let it be known that although some of the language is theirs, any irreverent attitude is solely that of the author.

I want to thank a few extraordinary people who were with me from the inception to completion of the book. There is Denise O'Sullivan, the kind of talented editor all writers want. And friend and writer, Phillip M. Perry, the kind of un-official editor all writers need. There is agent Julian Bach, who needs no help from *How to Talk to Anybody About Anything* because he already captivates the world conversationally. As for another friend who didn't need one word of English to convince me to write the book—thank you Captain Giorgio Accornero, for saying *"Tu devi scriverlo!"*

I am grateful to my ex-husband and current best friend, Barry Farber, for his rare devoted-divorcé's help. And of course to my publisher Steven Schragis who is wise enough to follow his heart and his gut in choosing books for publication.

Preface

An ace tennis player starting with a new partner knows what kind of game it's going to be just by watching the opponent's opening serve. Likewise, people can tell whether a conversation with you will be interesting and worthwhile, or a waste of time, just from your opening question.

It's not unusual to meet dozens of new people every week. Sought-after men and women must quickly judge who is worthy of their valuable time to whom they will give business, friendship, and even love a chance to blossom.

Every book on good communication echoes Dale Carnegie's wisdom on good rapport. In *How to Win Friends and Influence People* he tells us to make others feel important by showing knowledgeable interest in them.

This pivotal point of the other books is the opening premise *How to Talk to Anybody About Anything*. It picks up where they leave off, and provides you with the precise questions to make new acquaintances feel important by getting them to talk about themselves and their interests.

How to Talk to Anybody About Anything is the advanced course in communication. It is for people who wish to become masters in meeting people, making friends, and creating rapport. It's for people who, at a social gathering, want to start intelligent conversation with, say, the scientist, the architect, the psychiatrist, or the clergyperson seated a few feet away. And then continue chatting knowledgeably as the subject leaps from bowling, computers, chess, and cooking—to astrology, yoga, and wine. It's also for wise business people who know that getting the account often depends on good boat talk or tennis talk with the client.

How to Talk to Anybody About Anything is a unique exploration of the English language and how to use its subtleties to your advantage. It is a dictionary of conversational literacy in question format, or what I like to call a *conversationary*.

Without burdening you with esoteric jargon, the book improves your conversational skills and helps you overcome awkward encounters. You will not bluff more knowledge than you have about a particular trade, subject, or hobby. But just as a woman chooses the correct color lipstick or a man selects the right tie, you will choose appropriate opening conversation to enhance your image and set the stage for more interesting and meaningful communication.

How to Use This Book

Just as you need a map to travel through unknown cities, you need guidance to ask intelligent questions about a field you may not be familiar with.

Obviously, upon being introduced to strangers, you're not going to whip the book out of your pocket or purse, look up their interest, and read them the questions. But a casual reading beforehand familiarizes you with over a hundred new worlds. When you have a basic understanding of what is important to others, the right questions come to mind naturally.

Each chapter proceeds logically, like conversation. First there are several questions called "ice breakers" to get you over the initial conversational hurdles in an unfamiliar field. These are the typical insider's openers—the type that architects ask architects, kayakers ask kayakers, and cowboys ask cowboys. They are the same questions I heard insiders asking each other over and over during the hours, days, and sometimes weeks I immersed myself in their various worlds. I chose logical questions which do not depend on heavy jargon, so they are easy to remember.

When appropriate, we move on to more sophisticated and thoughtful queries. Almost every profession, every interest, has its ongoing hot issues that "everybody" is buzzing about. Industry conventions and trade journals are teeming with discussions of these important matters, but outsiders remain ignorant of them—until now. For these questions, I spoke with the groups' most prominent leaders—association presidents, communications directors, and top editors at the major trade publications.

So that you are not just throwing out questions, and to enable you to continue discussing their heartfelt concerns, the book gives you background information with each question. These deeper questions are designed to spawn philosophical musings from your new acquaintance and turn small talk into big talk. They're the type of on-target queries that form the foundation for a fast friendship.

When you know ahead of time the professions or interests of the people you are going to meet, you can review the appropriate chapters and brush up on specific conversational strategies. The entries are organized alphabetically so that you can look up the field you want to converse in as easily as you would a word in a dictionary.

Finally, a note on a couple of small words with big implications: To avoid burdening the reader throughout the book with the unwieldy *he or she,* if there are currently more men or women in a particular field, I use the corresponding pronoun more often.

A Word on Words

I was aware of the need for this book as far back as I can remember. As a kid I made the painful discovery that using certain words with the gang tagged me an outsider and using others made me more popular, an insider.

We're not so very different as adults. Saying the word *shop* instead of *agency* when talking with an advertising person establishes subconscious rapport. As does saying *firm* with a lawyer, saying *house* with a publisher, or asking an architect which *office* he or she works with. Unfair? Arbitrary? Exclusionary? Probably, but people are sensitive about words that describe their lives. And I must admit I enjoy the warm smile and heartfelt handshake that result from a sense of shared interests.

Our extraordinary language is rich in subtext and innuendo. Those proficient in this subtle skill can open doors that are closed to their less eloquent (or glib) fellow Americans. For instance, it's rude to ask a rock musician if he plays the piano well. But you've made a friend when you ask, "How are your chops?" Same question, different words, different impact.

Expert communication is becoming an enormous challenge. It's not just asking the right questions. It's asking them using the right words—and avoiding the wrong ones. In our increasingly specialized society, every subculture, every profession, trade, sport, and hobby has developed its own friendly and unfriendly words.

For example, people who play squash or watch birds feel rapport with you when they hear their words, *squasher* or *birder,* roll easily off your tongue. Conversely, boat owners consider you an outsider if you call their boat *it* instead of *she.* A pharmacist feels you are empathetic to his or her whole universe of professional problems when you say *community pharmacy* instead of *drugstore.*

Some people think striving for politically correct language has gone too far, but chiropractors warm to new acquaintances who call them *chiropractic doctors.* And veterinarians are apt to tune out people who call them *vets.*

How to Talk to Anybody About Anything highlights these and many supposedly arbitrary small words, which are not small or arbitrary at all. Enthusiasts speak of *owning* horses, *keeping* fish, or *having* cats. The verbs are not interchangeable to devotees. It is remarkable how using one uncustomary preposition, verb, or abbreviation can label you as unsympathetic with another's world. For example, saying that a person in a wheelchair *is disabled,* rather than *has a disability,* tags you as insensitive.

Tactful armchair conversation jocks know never to utter the ghastly words *fall, crash,* or *die* when talking with thrill-sport adventurers. (You needn't learn their euphemisms for "fatal accident," but a rock climber *craters,* a hang glider *goes in,* a bungee jumper *splats,* and a skydiver *bounces*—obviously only once).

In other sports, there are happier words which are music to the participants' ears. A backpacker smiles when you say *wilderness* instead of *woods;* kayakers prefer *paddling* to *rowing.*

The suggested questions use these key terms and particular usages of common words that establish subliminal rapport. The book strictly avoids esoteric jargon and, if any unfamiliar lingo is necessary, I explain the term, put it in context, and make it usable. I also point out passé phrases which might label you as out of touch with your new friend's way of thinking, such as the words *New Ager* and *pleasure boating.*

Our rich language has also developed special insiders' greetings. Actresses warm to well-wishers who say "Break a leg!" before a show; runners feel kinship with those who say, "Have a personal best!"; and firefighters feel you're a soulmate when, instead of "So long," you say, "See you at the big one!"

How to Talk to Anybody About Anything is the only book ever written which explores these and many other subtleties of respectful and intimate communication. Use the book as your key to unlock the glass doors that many sought-after people must close around themselves. Naturally, once you've passed through the doors and made new friends, continuing good communication is up to you.

Talking With Accountants

The accountant. No matter how dashing and debonair she is on the surface, we always assume that underneath, an unromantic dullard is crying to get out and bore us. We figure when a CPA hears, "How do I love thee, let me count the ways," it's the counting part that interests him.

Their job seems monotonous and the least fun in the world. What kid ever played accountant? Even if he wanted to grow up to be one.

So stifle your yawn, hold the bean-counting jokes, and pose the following questions. Then quickly get on to some more interesting aspect of his life. Maybe he bungee jumps or drives a flashy sports car.

Accountants have been known to stop at nothing in futile attempts to crush their green-eyeshade, rolled-shirtsleeves, number-crunching, crashing-bore image.

ICEBREAKERS

Are You in Public Practice?
The minute you say *public practice*, he will assume you share a vision of the world through green-colored eyeshades. *Public* practice, in AccountantSpeak, means serving the public, working in an accounting firm or as a *sole practitioner*. Accountants in the *private* sector work in industry. The terms are understandably baffling to those who only have reluctant annual discourse, in April, with an accountant.

Another possibility is that he or she works in government or academia, two other entities that need Herculean help in balancing the books.

Do You Specialize in Any Particular Type of Clients or Industries?

Pose this question to the accountant in public practice. He expects a little gasp of awe if he tells you he works for one of the *big six*—the six largest, and most prestigious, accounting firms.

Are You Active in Any State or National Associations?

Unless the statisticians are cooking the books, two out of three accountants participate in association activities. Invite him to crow a little by asking if he does any *committee work*.

You Must Have Uncovered Some Pretty Interesting Situations During the Course of Your Engagement With Your Clients.

To put a little more passion and pizzazz in their profession, accountants don't just work for clients, they have *engagements* with them.

Speak his language and he'll roll down his sleeves and regale you with insiders' stories. It's a rare accountant who cannot tell tales of the unfathomable creativity and depths to which the human imagination has dug to conjure up filthy money laundering scams.

Have You Been Affected by the Liability Phenomenon?

Bingo! You're hitting the single biggest issue menacing his industry today. CPA firms are beginning to bear the brunt of monumental suits for unlucky tax advice, or so-called *faulty audits*. Any accountant who audits a public company may be targeted for a suit.

Is the High Cost of Malpractice Insurance Hitting Accountants as Well as Doctors?

This one's best for the sole practitioner. His or her answer will be a loud yes, but your insightful query will invite a passionate recounting of the long version.

How Do You Feel About the Unfair Image of Your Profession?
This question makes you a kindred soul. Accountants' associations pay public relations pros a fortune to quash their dreaded pencil-pushing, bean-counting, book-cooking image.

Special thanks to Jeff Pickard, Vice President for Communications, American Institute of Certified Public Accountants, and James Craig, Managing Editor, *The CPA Journal,* New York, New York

Talking With Actors and Actresses

It seems the English-speaking world agrees, on both sides of the Atlantic, how to tell an actor from us ordinary mortals. British actor Michael Wilding once said, "You can pick out the actors by the glazed look that comes into their eyes when the conversation wanders away from themselves." Marlon Brando translates: "An actor's a guy who, if you ain't talking about him, ain't listening."

Obviously Messers Wilding and Brando didn't frequent the faux-chic restaurants dotting New York and L.A. The waiter and waitress, usually aspiring entertainers, actually listen—after giving a melodramatic reciting of tonight's specials—to your menu choice.

Those who do not dine where performers work to support their acting habit can, however, bask in their radiance for free. Legions of young dreamers perform on the streets of every major city in order to shut out bankruptcy and the blues.

The following compassionate questions are for the 95 percent of performers who are *between engagements* 90 percent of the time. Tallulah Bankhead summed it all up: "If you really want to help the American theater, don't be an actress, dahling. Be an audience."

4

ICEBREAKERS

Do You Do Community or Professional Theater?
This nonthreatening question is a sensitive opener unless your new friend is a performer in New York, Los Angeles, or possibly Chicago. In the Big Apple, La La Land, and Big Windy, assume their involvement is professional.

Do You Do Mostly Film or Stage?
That's how the theater crowd asks their fellow thespians if they're waiting by the phone for TV and movie producers to call or holding their breath for theater producers.

In general, West Coast performers pursue TV and film roles. East Coast professionals do more *live theater* and work in daytime television soap operas, or *the soaps*.

If he or she has a specialty like *voice overs*, or making animal noises, or is gifted with an adorable sneeze—a much-in-demand talent for cold remedy commercials—the performer will let you know.

Never ask the *artist* for a sample performance. Even a seemingly effortless sneeze is a contrived creative achievement.

Do You Do Mostly Musicals or Straight Plays?
This is the insider's way of asking stage performers if they sing and dance as well as act. Someone who does all three is known *in the biz* as a *triple threat.*

If you are talking with a singer, ask, "Do you do mostly *clubs* or *shows?*" Leave it to the singer to tell you if he or she *has an act* or is, perhaps, in a chorus.

What Types of Roles Have You Been Cast In?
More compassionate by far than "What have you done?" Remember you're dealing with an ego that is constantly bruised by agents, producers, and insensitive relatives who don't recognize true genius. You might also ask, "What have some of your favorite roles been?"

Are You in Anything Now?
Ask this question only if you assume the answer is yes. If she tells you she is *in rehearsal*, follow up with questions like . . .

How Are Rehearsals Going? and **When Do You Open?**
If you get the idea she's not, well, in anything just now, change that question to . . .

What Are You Working On?
Don't expect her to tell you that what she's really working on is figuring how to pay the rent.

How Did You Prepare for That Role?
Because most people only talk with an actor or actress during the "meet the cast" hour after a show, it is absolutely imperative that the first words out of your mouth be something appreciative about his performance. And don't say how wonderful he was to be able to "memorize all those lines."

When you decide you want deep communication with the rising star, let the youngest thespians regale you with stories about their *craft*. Ask them *who they study under* and what *techniques* they use.

Let the older ones tell you how bad this season has been for everyone in the biz and of their high hopes for the latest *audition*.

Leave it to the oldest few to reflect on the state of the performing arts in America today ("it's the pits"), and to tell you *what they did for love*.

A final word of warning: It's a bad omen to say "good luck" to a performer before a show. The superstitious show biz crowd always says, "*Break a leg!*"

For directors, producers, filmmakers, playwrights, screenwriters, and a host of other creative types:

Are You Working on Any Project Now? or **Tell Me About Your Latest Project.**
Ego runs high in this sincerely insincere and securely insecure, mad, mad bicoastal world of show business. Only one thing remains constant, the word *project*. This all-inclusive term covers everything from tiny home video documentaries to big-budget films, backers' auditions in a barn to Broadway shows. The salutations for them are:
For film folk: "*See you at the Oscars!*"
For television people: "*See you at the Emmys!*"
For theater types: "*See you at the Tonys!*"

Special thanks to Stefan Fitterman, Assistant to the President, Actors' Equity Association, and David Sheward, Managing Editor, *Backstage* magazine, New York, New York.

Talking With Advertising People

People drawn to advertising are a reasonably artistic lot. But alas, a few weeks into the job, they develop an irreversible work-related illness. They begin craving the luxuries they convince others they can't live without. And to afford them, they must plug their creative electricity into the corporate socket.

Nevertheless, they do it with their usual flair. When a client tells them to jump, they not only ask "How high?" but also "When should I come down?"

Naturally such ostentatious groveling takes its toll on these sensitive souls. You'll hear the *creative people* crying in their champagne that they've sold out.

ICEBREAKERS

Are You With an Agency?
The adman and adwoman's instinctive opener. The advertising person may work *in-house* for a large corporation or in an advertising agency, which he or she will casually refer to as *the shop*.

8

Which Shop Are You With?

The word *shop* sliding smoothly between your lips alerts ad folk that you are comfortably conversant with their world.

Ask ad agency types, "What department do you work in?" This discloses whether they are among the lofty *creative people* like the *copywriters* who write the ads or the *art directors* who plan the visuals. (See the artists chapter for additional questions for art directors.)

Another possibility is *account executive*—*account exec* for short. These are the business acrobats who can suspend themselves in midair for clients longer than anyone else.

At many shops there is a cleft between the creative and the account people.

Do You Do Mostly Print or TV?

You've just asked whether she works on ads for magazines, newspapers, and billboards, or on television commercials.

A few insider's terms: When you are talking about print work, refer to the pictures as *art* and the words as *copy*. If you start talking television, vary the word *commercial* with *spot*.

What Accounts Are You Working On?

AdSpeak for "Which clients' commercials are you working on?" If you've seen one of the sponsor's television commercials, ask your new friend if she worked on that ad or spot. In the mood for a long story? Ask for details about how and where it was *shot*.

What Are Some of Your Favorite Campaigns?

Campaign is the key word here. You've invited him to tell you about the series of commercials he most enjoyed working on.

Does Your Shop Do Any Public Service?

A chivalrous query to help alleviate the dream merchant's

guilt. Most large advertising agencies do a few free commercials for worthy causes. The creative types enjoy the welcome break from weaving whole lies out of half-truths. They also feel they can expose the world to more of their artistic genius through these less client-controlled *PS* spots.

Special thanks to Jeff Custer, Director of Media Relations, American Advertising Federation, Washington, D.C.

Talking With Aerobics Enthusiasts

"Basically," to quote one of the world's foremost cardiovascular exercise experts, "aerobics is getting up off your duff and moving around to get the heartbeat up."

Back in the fifties only sports coaches and army sergeants endorsed it, and then it was only to win or kill better. But today every gymnasium worth a drop of sweat has highly touted aerobics classes.

Many a sedentary intellectual, seated next to an exercise monomaniac at dinner parties, has suffered in silence while the aerobics enthusiast pecks at a lettuce leaf and gives an unsolicited monologue on the importance of exercise.

The following will, at least, transform the evening into a dialogue.

ICEBREAKERS

Do You Do Low Impact or High Impact?
A *high-impact* class lasts about an hour and consists almost entirely of jumping and hopping. Because some enthusiasts feel high-impact aerobics puts a great strain on the knee joints, they devised *low-impact*. A low-impact routine allows one foot to always be on the floor. An aerobic workout is achieved by swinging, swaying, stepping, and thrashing arms around a lot more instead.

11

A combination of the two, *high-low-impact*, is also very popular.

How Hard Do You Work Out? and How Long Do You Work Out?

If you're talking with an aerobics instructor, substitute fancier terms like *frequency*, *duration*, and *intensity*.

Do You Use Any Equipment in Your Workout?

We're talking an assortment of gizmos like rubber stretch bands, leg weights, small dumbbells, rubber balls, and possibly a few portable steps for *step classes*.

Do You Do Any Cross Training?

You're asking if there are any other disciplines like *stretching* or *body sculpting* incorporated into his or her routine.

Do You Do It Primarily for Cardiovascular Fitness or to Keep Trim?

Shows you're no couch potato. If you feel more comfortable, simply ask, "What *results* do you expect to get from your classes?"

Special thanks to John Poteet, Associate Director of Continuing Education, Cooper Institute for Aerobics Research, Dallas, Texas.

Talking With Aircraft Owners and Private Pilots

Airmen and airwomen are really down-to-earth folks. They're no different from the rest of the gang shopping at the mall or munching a fast-food hamburger. But don't expect to see these semi-high fliers on weekends. They're buzzing around overhead in their little cloud busters. In the time it takes to drive to the nearest McDonald's, they're at some airport canteen, many miles away, munching on what the *private pilot* gleefully calls the (wink-wink, nudge-nudge), "hundred-dollar hamburger."

ICEBREAKERS

What Type of Airplane Do You Fly?
You can drop your final *g*'s and slur your diphthongs when talking with an *airman*, but you must pronounce both syllables of *air-plane*. Shortening it to "plane" tags you as a know-nothing landlubber.

Next query is, "Do you fly your airplane for business or pleasure?"

What Ratings Do You Have?
Pilot to pilot this is a must-ask question. There are three basic ratings. A *private pilot* can take you up in his little tree-trimmer. A *commercial pilot* is permitted to fly larger aircraft

13

for hire. And an *air transport pilot's license* means he's succumbed to *big iron fever* and has a rating that allows him to fly for an airline.

How Much Flying Time Do You Have?

He will tell you in hours. Ask also, "Where do you fly?" and "Have you ever flown out of the country?"

Do You Have Your Instrument Rating Yet?

This is a question for new pilots only. After getting her *private pilot's certificate*, she goes for an *instrument rating* so she can fly in clouds and on *marginal weather* days.

Where Do You Base Your Airplane?

The key word here is *base*. Such imprecise terms as "keep" or "store" show that you're not one of the prop set. If he rents rather than owns an airplane, ask, "Where do you fly out of?"

Were You a Military Pilot?

Save this one for older fliers. Uncle Sam gave many private pilots their start.

Ever Have to Make Any Forced Landings?

Invitation to story hour, pilot-style.

How Serious Has the Product Liability Situation Become?

In a word, very. But let the experienced pilot sound off on this major concern in the industry. Liability insurance costs have skyrocketed because manufacturers are still responsible for airplanes made twenty, thirty, even forty years ago. As a result, they only make a limited number of airplanes, which drives costs up for the new buyer.

What's Your Favorite Weekend Fly-in?

Fliers love to talk about their *weekend fly-ins.* But it's a big boner to call him or her a "weekend pilot."

For professional airline pilots: **Whom Do You Fly For?** *etc.* Once he crawls out of the cockpit, all questions in the flight attendants chapter concerning *layovers, bidding for routes, travel privileges,* and *airline deregulation* are your boarding pass to great conversation with a professional pilot.

Special thanks to Thomas B. Haines, Executive Editor, *AOPA Pilot,* Aircraft Owners and Pilots Association, Frederick, Maryland

Talking With Amateur Radio Enthusiasts (Hams)

If you ask a *ham* where the name comes from, he or she will tell you, as solemnly as a mother hog educating her little piglets, all about the word. Some contend that when the British couldn't quite pronounce *ams* for "amateur radio" enthusiasts, they became known as *hams*. Others say it's due to the "ham-fisted" way some early radio amateurs punched their Morse code keys.

But if the truth were known, it's probably just because amateur two-way radio operators love "hamming" it on the airwaves.

ICEBREAKERS

What Kind of Radio Do You Do?

This is ham shorthand for three questions: "Whom do you talk to?" "What do you talk about?" and "For what purpose (if any)?"

A loquacious lot, hams like to gab with each other around the clock, around the country, and around the globe, on their high-frequency radio bands. Some just chat with people in other states or in other neighborhoods on little pocket radios clipped to their belts, called *HTs* for *Handie-Talkies*. (Don't call them "walkie-talkies." That's kid stuff.)

What's Your License Class?

A crucial ham-to-ham query. There are five *license classes*. In increasing order of difficulty, they are *novice, technician, general, advanced,* and *amateur extra.* The higher you go, the more tests, the more privilege, and the more time-consuming and obsessive the hobby becomes.

Can You Explain Your Call Sign to Me?

The boys in the high bands are assigned a *sign* consisting of various letters and numbers. These reveal where they're from and when their license was issued.

A word of caution. Do *not* say "ten-four" or "good buddy" to a ham. That's CB talk. Hams are more civilized than their unlicensed, unruly CB mates. So they tell me.

Ask CBers, "What's your *handle?*" (radio name)

Also, don't get hams mixed up with *scanners.* Scanners only listen. The crucial scanner question is, "What *channels* do you listen to?" The channels can be airlines, police—anything.

Have You Ever Been a Control Operator?

During busy times, a volunteer *control operator* routes the calls of other hams—sort of like a switchboard operator.

Have You Been Involved in Any Emergency Activities?

A welcome question indeed. Radio amateurs are proud that the Federal Communications Commission calls upon *radio operators* to help save lives and property during emergencies and natural disasters. They often refer to their hobby as a *service.* During earthquakes, floods, hurricanes, blizzards, and other dramatic disasters, ham ears round the world are glued to their radios.

Special thanks to Steve Mansfield, Public Information Manager, American Radio Relay League, Newington, Connecticut.

Talking With Aquarium Hobbyists

Fishkeeping is a lazy pet-lover's hobby. You don't pet fish, groom them, train them, spay them, or take them for walks. And you certainly don't need to bathe them. Just pitch a fingerful of daily fish food, and blow them a kiss before turning out the lights, right?

And wake up the next day to a tank full of dead fish.

Successful *aquarists* work hard. They struggle to find just the right balance of gravel, plants, heat, light, filtering, and chemicals for treating the water. And if they don't do it right, the fish have the nerve to die on them. The finickiest cat wouldn't give its owner an ultimatum like that.

ICEBREAKERS

What Kind of Fish Do You Keep? or **Do You Keep a Salt Water or Fresh Water Tank?**
Mentioning the two options displays your remarkable awareness of the difference between the two hobbies. Saltwater fish are colorful but much more fragile in captivity.

If the hobbyist has a *saltwater tank*, show you know the usual aquarist's progression by asking, "Did you start with a *freshwater tank?*"

How Big Are Your Tanks?

Home hobbyists' tanks vary from little ten-gallon starter tanks to room-size. Be impressed if his or her tank is over a hundred gallons.

Do You Have a Good Dealer?

Unlike those whose pets don't have the nasty habit of dying, fishkeepers must stay in constant contact with a dealer for new fish, new equipment, advice, and lots of consolation.

Do You Keep a Community Tank or a Species Tank?

In a *community tank* several species live (and die) together. A *species* tank is one species only.

Ask also, "Do all your fish swim happily together?" In other words, "Are they becoming territorial, greedy, and swallowing each other up?"

Do You Try to Breed Your Fish?

If yes, you're talking to an expert. Manipulating the erotic whims of fish is a greater challenge than arousing rabbits.

Do You Keep Live Plants in Your Tank?

If he or she *keeps* a saltwater tank, also called a *marine tank*, keeping plants in it can be difficult. Also ask about *coral* and *anemones* in the tank.

How Long Have You Been Able to Keep Your Fish Going?

This is the aquarist's euphemism for, "How long can you keep your fish before they go gills up?"

Special thanks to Ed Bauman, Senior Editor, *Aquarium Fish Magazine*, Mission Viejo, California; and Mark Hawver, Supervisor, Advertising and Promotion, Tetra Home Aquarium Products, Morris Plains, New Jersey.

Talking With Architects

Have you ever pondered where the saying, "Well, back to the drawing board" comes from? Obviously, it was first uttered by a frustrated young architect.

"The doctor can bury his mistakes," Frank Lloyd Wright observed, "but an architect can only advise his clients to plant vines." Many vines later, the argument of form versus function still rages on. Architects still dream of creating the ultimate structure—an inhabitable sculpture that "works." In order to accomplish that, they must find mistakes on the drawing board before those mistakes become immortalized in concrete.

ICEBREAKERS

Where Is Your Office Located? or **What's the Size of Your Office?**
Firm is acceptable, but architect to architect, it's *office*.

Why? Architects like to feel their place of work is less corporate than a "law firm," more artistic than a supplier's "company," and more levelheaded than an artist's "studio."

Do You Specialize in Certain Building Types or Areas of Design?
A simple architectural refinement on "What's your specialty?"

What Types of Projects Have You Been Involved In?

The key word is *project.* Also ask what project he has found most interesting. And of course ask about the current project.

Do You Find Various State Regulations Are Eroding Your Profession?

Absolutely! Architects feel the heat from state registration and licensing boards, and from political pressure. Some of the heat results from a much stronger engineering profession.

Is It Getting More Difficult to Do Your Job Because of All the Interference?

Architects will know exactly what, and whom, you're talking about—construction managers, interior designers, contract inspectors, and a host of other intruders. Various areas of specialization keep eating away at the role of the architect. They will tell you it is especially irritating because their education is broader in scope than that of the munchers.

Do You Find Yourself Faced With Many Constraints on Your Current Project?

Today's architect must satisfy a lot of people in addition to himself and his client. You're expressing sensitivity to this plight when you ask about *client, code,* or *budget* constraints on the current *project.*

Do You Find Yourself Moving into Kinds of Work You Hadn't Anticipated?

Older architects seldom get to live in the career castles they designed in their youth. They bemoan the fact that society no longer looks upon the architect as the "master builder."

Special thanks to Stanley Banash, Executive Director, Society of American Registered Architects, Lombard, Illinois.

Talking With Artists

Every child is an artist. "The problem," Pablo Picasso said, "is how to remain one, once he grows up." It isn't clear whether Picasso was talking about the difficulty of retaining one's creativity or the dilemma of how to be an artist and pay the rent.

Many a penniless artist has faced a demanding landlord and pleaded, "But I'm an *artist.* Someday tourists will be pointing at your building and saying, 'That great abstract painter used to live here.' " To which landlords shrug and reply, "And if you don't pay up, they can come by tomorrow and say that."

Problems aside, anyone who can live off his art should wake up every day and kiss the canvas he paints on. Art is its own reward. And deep down, every artist knows it.

ICEBREAKERS

What Medium Do You Work In?

By asking about materials, you avoid sounding like you are asking the artist to describe his or her work. Many artists feel that their work cannot, or should not, be translated into words.

Examples of a *medium* are acrylics, oil, charcoal, or pen. If the artist is a *crafts person, graphics artist, sculptor, graffiti artist,* or even *performance artist,* he or she will tell you.

Are You a Commercial Artist or a Fine Artist? or **Do You Illustrate or Are You a Painter?**

The second is a more casual way to ask the same question of a *visual artist,* one who paints or draws.

Fine artists might think of themselves as creating art for art's sake and pride themselves on total freedom of expression. *Commercial* artists work for clients and might pride themselves on interpreting someone else's vision and on being able to pay the rent.

Can You Spend Much Time in Your Studio?

A sensitive way to ask if he or she is a full-time artist or must take another job to support the art habit.

If your new friend is admittedly a struggling artist, an appropriate question is "How do you think an artist's financial situation influences his or her art, or does it?" There are those who feel that the best art is produced by artists who can stay in their studio all day and work. Others prefer the cliché that great art comes from starving artists.

For Fine Artists: **Do You Like to Show Your Work, or Do You Paint (Sketch) Primarily for Yourself?**

A further exploration of your new friend's art involvement. Also ask the fine artist . . .

Is It Absolutely Necessary Nowadays to Be Affiliated With a Gallery?

Artists are heartened that some gallery guides now list unaffiliated artists who *show* in their own studios.

This question also smokes out whether your new friend's work hangs in a gallery. If so, follow up with "Are you represented exclusively by one gallery, or do you have your pieces in a number of galleries?"

"Whom have you shown with?" often reveals what caliber of artist your new friend is in the eyes of the world.

For Commercial Artists: **Is There Anywhere I Might Have Seen Your Work?**
This is a gentle way to ask about their markets. Another is "What type of clients do you work for?"

For Graphics Artists: **Are You Using a Computer? and Do You Do Your Own Output?**
Graphics artists are commercial artists who work primarily with layout, lettering, and design. The old days of *pasting up mechanicals* are gone, and almost all graphics artists now work on computer. The result, *output* or *hard copy*, requires expensive equipment. Many artists have to take their work to a shop to get the output.

The following questions are for all types of artists:

Are There Any Regions That Are More Receptive to Your Work Than Others?
How perceptive of you to be aware of regional tastes.

How Do You Feel About How Your Art Is Interpreted?
This question is especially relevant for established artists whose work is often reviewed. Some artists feel that art stands alone and cannot be interpreted. Others accept it as one of the realities of the art business.

What Is Your Feeling About Mega-Events?
There is much disagreement whether an event with long lines of ticket holders to see piles of Picasso or mounds of Matisse brings art to the masses or is an obscenity.

What Do You Think the 1980s Did—or Undid—for Art?
Be sure to add "or undid" to show your awareness that the 1980s were very market-driven. Many artists feel that the decade produced art not for the ages but for the whims of investors and status seekers and that the outrageous prices

did damage. You might like to argue one side of the issue, "Did all that attention (for the wrong reasons?) seize art away from the masses and damage the market for unknown artists—or not? Few would claim that the decade gave the world a single major artist, but ask.

Now That We're at the End of Another Century, What Do You Think We Can Say About This One?
Art historians make generalizations at every *fin de siècle* on how the thought, culture, and philosophy of the century is reflected in its art. Essentially, you are asking the unanswerable question, "What is the contemporary art world?" But your new friend, the artist, might like to give it a whirl.

I Realize That It's Unthinkable to Ask an Artist to Characterize His Work, but . . .
Naturally you've been dying to ask what your new friend's art is like, but most artists become ill at the thought of verbal descriptions. This question shows your sensitivity, and it will merit you the best answer the artist is willing to give you.

Other ways to circumvent the invasive question are "Whose work do you really like?" and "Whose work inspired you when you were just starting?" The answers tell a lot about the artist.

If you're intent on getting a more specific answer, you can give a little coaching, like, "Would you say your work is more abstract, or conceptual . . . hmmm?"

But be careful. You must use a light brush on the eggshells of an artist's ego.

Special thanks to Fergus Reid, Editor, *Art Business News*, Stamford, Connecticut; and Michael Ward, Editorial Director, *Artists* magazine and the Art Magazine Group, Cincinnati, Ohio.

Talking With Astrology Buffs

The next time an intense stargazer demands to know what sign you are, you needn't obediently comply and then subject yourself to his or her mysterious, mumbled, "Hmm, I thought so."

Here is a gracious reversal of the interrogation, which turns inquisitor into defendant, and shows that you're no cosmic turkey.

ICEBREAKERS

Do You Follow the Planets Professionally or as a Hobby?
Referring to *the planets* rather than "the stars" is an obvious demonstration of your psychic superiority.

Do You Do Other People's Charts?
A question for the hobbyist. *Doing* clients' *charts* and *giving readings* is the professional astrologer's job.

Clients consult astrologers for spiritual growth and development, for insight into their karmic destiny patterns, and to help them get more money, power, and sex. Astrological services are called *future prediction, character analysis,* and *counseling.*

Do You Make Specific Plans in Your Own Life Based on Your Readings?
Go gently; you're asking if they actually believe their own

26

predictions. Any visionary who is not a total charlatan will, of course, use astrology as a guideline. But ask about the influence of predictions on specific temporal exigencies like dates of important meetings and financial investments in his or her own life.

Do You Think the Sun Sign or the Rising Sign Is More Important?

The *sun sign,* determined by birth date, is the sign touted in the horoscope column of romance magazines and grocery store weeklies. Serious astrologers also explore the *rising sign,* which involves not only the date but the place and time of birth.

What Role Do You Feel Free Will Plays in Astrology?

Even astrologers argue among themselves whether astrology reveals what is predetermined or whether there is free will involved. Ask for an opinion.

Then sit back and figure how much free will you can exercise in changing the subject.

Special thanks to Ken Irving, Editor, *American Astrology,* New York, New York.

Talking With (Professional) Athletes

Athletes who have achieved the heights, no matter what the sport, have certain qualities in common. Verbal articulation and an air of intelligence may not be among them. But let's include motivation, self-discipline, personal goal setting, and a host of other nonphysical attributes.

When talking with a professional athlete, most people focus their questions on the big competitions. But unless you know all about his sport, the names of his team members, his complete performance record, and the name of his first hometown coach, don't attempt it.

Ask, rather, these questions—designed for the complete sports illiterate—which concentrate on the more cerebral aspects of the sport. The athlete will find your questions provocative and preferable by far to the usual hackneyed fawning.

ICEBREAKERS

What Kind of Mental Training Do You Do?
Athletes use an intriguing array of psychological techniques to get themselves in *peak performance* for a game or competition. *Imagery* is one of them, by which the mind's eye sees the body accomplish a certain task. Other techniques are

relaxation training and *stress inoculation,* which makes the body sense the game pressure ahead of time.

What's Your Usual Preperformance Routine?

Another way of asking this is "Do you have any techniques for getting yourself really *focused* for a game (competition or match)?"

Successful athletes have discovered what personally works for them before a big game or competition. It might be meditation, listening to heavy metal music, or going over a game book.

When discussing this desired pregame state, avoid the common phrase "getting psyched up." Athletes like to think more in terms of being *focused, in control,* or *energized.*

Is There Anything Specific You're Working on in Practice (or Training) Now?

This question shows your appreciation of the way professional athletes challenge *themselves.* They're continually setting short-term realistic goals that they must accomplish.

What Do You Do to Get Your Mind Off the Game?

Athletes have a tendency to be obsessive about their sport, but they realize it's not constructive. This question may lead into some other aspects of the athlete's life that you'll both enjoy exploring.

Special thanks to Dr. Shane Murphy, Chairperson, Athletic Performance Division, U.S. Olympic Committee, Colorado Springs, Colorado.

Talking With Backpackers

The stalwart backpacker, with everything he needs for comfort and survival strapped on his back, charges into the wilderness, self-contained and self-propelled. He's the captain of his ship, master of his fate—until the temperature plummets, he runs out of provisions, a thunderstorm strikes, or mosquitoes attack.

Experienced backpackers prepare themselves for these natural disasters and acts of God. They carry sweaters, an extra Hershey's bar, a rainproof parka, and plenty of canned chemical warfare to ward off attack from airborne adversaries.

By now their pack is getting pretty heavy, and it's no longer just a stroll in the woods. Backpacking is an ambulatory weight lifting competition and endurance test. Wilderness guys and gals thrive on it.

ICEBREAKERS

Do You Prefer Well-Established Trails, or Do You Like to Bushwhack?
Bushwhack or *cross country* means striking out in the wilderness, not necessarily following well-trodden trails. *Bushwhackers* thrive on pushing aside underbrush and making their own way.

A euphonic note. The words *wilderness* and *backcountry* are music to a serious backpacker's ears. Give him or her the pleasure by saying them whenever you can.

Do You Prefer Low-Elevation Hiking, or Do You Like to Go Above Tree Line?

Shows you're no city slicker. *Low-elevation* trekkers enjoy looking at vegetation and wildlife. The *above tree line* scramblers tend to be into hiking and backpacking more for the physical exercise and inspiring views from mountaintops.

What Kind of a Pack Do You Use?

Important stuff to a backpacker. There's a big difference between *internal frame* and *external frame* backpacks. Internal frame packs fit closer to the body, which helps *scramblers* keep their balance on steep terrain. External frames support heavier loads for long hikes on flatter trails.

What Gear Do You Carry in Your Backpack?

Backpackers will relish giving you a complete annotated inventory of everything they carry. Tiny tweezers may seem an insignificant addition, but it keeps a microscopic splinter from ruining an otherwise perfectly good outing. Hikers lie awake nights contemplating cosmic questions of weight versus possible necessity.

Do You Have a Tent or Do You Sleep Out Under the Stars?

If the overnight backpacker prefers only the sky for a ceiling, ask what kind of *fill* he or she has in the sleeping bag. More expensive *down feathers* are warmer but take longer to dry. Determined backpackers planning a drizzly adventure choose *synthetic fill.*

Some even carry tents on their backs and forgo hot showers and their favorite TV show for weeks on end. Hearty souls these backpackers.

Special thanks to Tom Shealey, Managing Editor, *Backpacker* magazine, Emmaus, Pennsylvania

Talking With (Hot Air) Balloonists

When you spot a tiny balloon pin on your new acquaintance's lapel, it shouts, "I've flown in a hot air balloon and am absolutely twitching to tell somebody all about it."

He or she will take your slightest acknowledgment as an invitation to sputter endlessly about the heavenly exhilaration of *riding the winds*. No destination, no time imperatives—except to stay afloat until the champagne is thoroughly chilled for the traditional postflight champagne brunch.

Balloonists, accused of being "rich, champagne-sipping wimps" by jocks and "thrill sport fanatics" by their more timid colleagues, don't really have an image. Nor do they care. They can afford not to.

ICEBREAKERS

Are You a Morning Person?
This question is deceivingly relevant. Most balloon rides take place in the early morning hours. Passengers and crew must be at the *launch site* by dawn in order to take off and catch the beauty of the sunrise.

Do You Go as Passenger, or Do You Pilot?
Ask if you suspect you're in the presence of an experienced

32

balloonist. Balloon *pilots* are skilled in judging wind conditions, manipulating altitude by heating trapped air, and avoiding obstacles during landings.

If you're talking with a pilot, ask his *rating*. The Federal Aviation Association licenses balloon pilots as *student, private,* or *commercial.*

Have You Ever Worked as Ground Crew (or Chase Crew)?

Many zealous balloonists are volunteer *crew*. Balloon *ground crew* (or *chase crew*) stay on terra firma. Their job is to jump in a truck or trailer and chase the balloon around some fifteen hundred feet below. Then they pack up the balloon—wherever the winds have taken it—and drive the euphoric passengers back to the champagne brunch.

Have You Had Any Interesting Flights (or Landings)?

Because the non-FAA-certified wind god Aeolus is the real pilot, the smoothness of the ride depends largely on his whims.

Even though, for passengers, the *sport* is just riding in the wicker *gondola*, there can be some *interesting* (upper-class for "lousy") landings. Ballooning is a rather safe diversion, however. Otherwise, moneyed folks wouldn't trust their substantial fates to the winds.

Do You Compete?

Save this one for very experienced balloonists. There are many balloon *rallies*, the world's largest being the annual *Albuquerque Balloon Fiesta.*

Your new balloon buddy will assume that you're no stranger to the lofty balloon set when you ask, "Do you go to *the* Balloon Fiesta?"

Special thanks to Doug Lane, Past President, and Sharon Ripperger, Executive Director, Balloon Federation of America, Indianola, Iowa; and Tom Hamilton, Publisher and Editor, *Balloon Life,* Sacramento, California.

Talking With Ballroom Dancers

Kids whose parents rescued them from drugs and cults in the seventies and eighties now wonder how to deliver Mom and Dad from *their* new addiction—social dancing.

All over the country, sound-of-body, over-forty types are sashaying off to ballrooms and shamelessly kicking up their heels dancing the fox-trot, polka, country, and the revolutionary old big band cheek to cheek, belly to belly.

It doesn't take much to get one of these mainliners to squeal. At the drop of a shoe, happy addicts will brainwash you about their "healthy form of social recreation with a little romance thrown in."

Watch out. Unless you can feign an ingrown toenail, one of these obsessive hoofers will abduct you and drag you off to a senior dance.

ICEBREAKERS

What Kind of Dancing Do You Do?
An obvious but welcome opener.

Do You Dance to Live Bands?
Those who do are passionate about it. You'll sorely disappoint them if you don't follow up with "Tell me about your favorite band."

Do You Dance in a Ballroom or a Studio?

In general, *ballroom* dancers thrive on the social aspect, whereas *studio* dancers concentrate more on technique. However, it's not just studios and ballrooms these hoofers prance around in. Got a barn? Let's have a dance.

Do You Take Lessons?

Ask this if Twinkle Toes has just discovered the joys of what they like to call *groovin' and duckin' around the room.* And say dance *instructor*, not "teacher."

Do You Enter Any Competitions? and Do You Perform?

Reserve these questions for seasoned swingers.

Do You Have a Regular Dancing Partner?

Many experienced dancers do, and they love perfecting their routines. If your new friend doesn't have a regular partner, it's time to start limping and complaining about your sore toe.

Special thanks to Doris Pease, Editor, *Dancing USA*, Minneapolis, Minnesota.

Talking With Bartenders

In the interest of charity and fair play, we will now have a short chapter dedicated to the pour man who is often nothing more to us than a sympathetic ear and a generous wrist. Incredible though it may seem, a bartender is a person too, with problems, a life, and a desire to talk to somebody about his world for a change.

Unlike some of their blue-collar or no-collar compatriots with self-anointed appellations like "nail technicians" and "sanitation specialists," a bartender chooses no ambitious titles. He's not a "mixologist" or "fizzical culturist." He's a *bartender*.

Bartenders will be friendly as long as you avoid the one question they dread, but alas, hear nightly, "So, what's your daytime job?" Many bartenders are lifetime professionals.

Their special job skills? They're experts in stereo listening—to you with one ear and the bar with the other. And they can cut off pie-eyed customers with an enviable gallantry.

ICEBREAKERS

How's Business?
The unalterable opener.

How Long Have You Been Behind the Stick (or Working the Wood)?
Ask this if you are curious to know how long he or she has been practicing the profession of pulling the seltzer stick.

You Must Have Some Great Full Moon Stories?
It's a scientific fact, as any longtime bartender will testify, that the full moon brings out the crazies. This question invites him to open his war story chest and regale you with tales of monthly fiascoes.

Who Are the Best Tippers? or Are Women Becoming Better Tippers?
A topic of some consequence to a bartender, whose major source of compensation can be gratuities.

To fortify you with some intriguing information: According to a recent survey on this vital matter, the worst tippers at bars are doctors, then lawyers, followed by schoolteachers. The best tippers are other workers who are paid by tips.

"Women" is the only category which has changed status in the past ten years. Women are rising up off the worst tippers list as more purses are seen lining the bars.

Special thanks to Ray Foley, Publisher, and Editor *Bartender* magazine, Livingston, New Jersey.

Talking With Bicyclists

The gang of little kids who buzzed around the old neighborhood on their Schwinns have given up their bubblegum but not their bikes. They have evolved into a generation of yuppies with expensive collections of *city bikes, mountain bikes, racing bikes,* and *touring bikes.*

They're everywhere. During the week, two-wheeled yuppies careen in front of your car in rush hour traffic, a purse or briefcase slung over their shoulders, a smug expression peeking out under tiny helmets. During weekend country drives, you spot clumps of them in the distance, their shiny black Spandex bottoms bouncing above bicycle seats on the horizon.

The number of bicyclists continues to grow as more nostalgic baby boomers enter second childhood. It is quite likely that you will soon find yourself in dialogue with a bikeaholic.

If you don't feel up to discussing the details of his or her derailleur, or debating side saddlebags versus backpacks, the following questions will successfully camouflage your shameful preference for automobiles.

ICEBREAKERS

What Kind of Cycling Do You Do?
This gets the *cyclist* started on whether he or she prefers *road riding* or *off-road cycling* on rugged trails.

What Kind of Bike Do You Have? or **Do You Have a Touring Bike or a Mountain Bike?**
Throwing out the two main alternatives hints that you're not a total stranger to pedaling.

The fat-wheeled *mountain bikes* (also called *all-terrain bikes* or *ATBs*) are more rugged for dirt trails. A must-ask for ATBers is, "Where are your favorite trails?"

Touring bikes are built for heavier loads and long distances on smoother surfaces. The lighter *racing bike* is built for greater speed.

Do You Use Your Bike for Commuting?
We see increasingly more Gucci pumps and loafers pumping away at bike pedals.

Do You Wear a Helmet?
A short question which can result in a long answer. Some strong opinions here.

Do You Join Any Organized Bike Tours? or **Have You Done Any Bicycling Vacations?**
All over the country, bicycle clubs sponsor charitable or recreational rides. Some enthusiasts pack up their bikes for a week and ride from one campsite or hotel to the next.

Do You Ride Mostly for Enjoyment or Exercise?
Most will say both. The cyclist will feel sportsman's kinship with you because you know that riding a bike is a terrific no-impact aerobic exercise and ecologically correct too. A double whammy.

Special thanks to Bob Ehrlich, Vice President for Operations, Bicycle Corporation of America, Bethlehem, Pennsylvania; and James McCullagh, Publisher, *Bicycling Magazine*, Emmaus, Pennsylvania.

Talking With Billiards and Pool Players

The old-style floor-spitting, cigar-sucking pool hustlers looking for a friendly dollar-a-point game may have to clean up their act. At least if they want to sink a few shots in the new upscale cool halls with espresso machines, no smoking areas, and art exhibitions. Chardonnay-sipping young professionals are discovering an old game and giving it new style.

If you find yourself behind the conversational eight-ball with one of these upscale, nouveau pool players, here are a few rescue shots.

ICEBREAKERS

What's Your Game?
A simple *break shot*. You might hear *three-cushion billiards, straight pool, snooker, eight-ball, nine-ball* . . .

The difference between *billiards* and *pool* continues to confound everyone who has never held a cue. The games are similar, except pool is played on a smaller table with pockets, and the most popular billiards is pocketless. The greater difference lies in the players' self-image. The billiards players consider themselves a higher caste.

What Kind of Cue Do You Have?
Even if the answer is confusing to you, this is a must-ask. You can always clarify it by asking what he or she likes about the *cue*. *Custom cues* are also very popular.
Players often ask, "What's your best shot?" *Banks, kicks, straight-ins,* and *cut shots* are just some of the names you might hear.

Do You Play in a League?
Or in a bar? You can also ask, "How good are you?" Ratings are simply *beginner, intermediate,* and *advanced.*

Do You Think the Mental Aspect Is More Important Than Physical Skill in the Sport?
A tad intellectual for the old-style pool player. But the new breed of pool yuppie will warm to your perceptive observation on the cerebral facet of the *sport.*
Minnesota Fats (back in the days when it was still a "game") would have said, "Nah, who ya kiddin'? Ninety percent of the game is half mental. The rest is in your head."

What Do You Think About So Many Women Getting Into the Sport?
The new sensitive male will give a politically correct, if not truthful, answer.

Special thanks to Debbie Huffman, Marketing and PR Director, Billiard Congress of America, Iowa City, Iowa; and Michael Panozzo, Editor, *Billiards Digest,* Chicago, Illinois.

Talking With Bird Watchers

With apologies to committed *birders* and ornithologists the world over, I anachronistically title this chapter "bird watchers." It's so their city cousins will know who we're talking about.

The term "bird watcher" is as passé as the Englishman in knickers and a monocle traipsing through marshes in hot pursuit of the elusive least bittern. Those who watch birds in this country call themselves *birders*. In the rest of the English-speaking world, they're *twitchers*.

An affluent lot, these *birders* and *twitchers*. Many a *big lister* has been known to drop everything but binoculars and gold credit card to follow his fine feathered friends halfway round the world.

ICEBREAKERS

What Got You Interested in Birding?
Always a proper opener. And you'll receive a proper answer, if you use the proper noun, *birding*.

Do You Feed Birds on Your Property?
In addition to following birds as far as their assets allow, most *committed birders* feed birds on their own estates. And they try ever so terribly hard to suppress feelings of superiority toward the *backyard feeder* who does no aggressive birding.

The backyard feeder's status comes up a notch, however, if his or her backyard has been registered by the United States Fish and Wildlife Service as a *wildlife habitat.* There are some ten million prestigious backyards bearing this coveted distinction.

How Elaborate Is Your Feeder?
For *feeders* only. Get ready to hear about exotic bird baths, oranges for seducing orioles, and nectar and sugar water for luring nightingales.

Do You Keep a Life List?
Serious stuff, these *life lists.* Most committed birders keep a lifelong list of their *sightings.* One who has *sighted* many species is nicknamed a *big lister* by envious colleagues.

Do You Photograph?
Many *birders* like to take pictures of the birds they spot. Few make tape recordings, however, as accidental replayings might cause the birds to have identity crises.

Birders, unlike hunters, are quite pleased with their status as *nonconsumptive* users of wildlife.

Special thanks to Eldon D Greij, Publisher and Editor, *Birders World,* Holland, Michigan

Talking With Boat Owners

A bewildered apology is offered to owners of sailboats, motorboats, and yachts, who, I am told, will find it odious to share even a chapter. Motorboat owners, like lovers of fast cars, delight in big engines. They speed past sailboats, *ragpickers* they call them, oblivious to the sailors who are glaring and muttering "ostentatious *stinkpotters*" and worse.

Laboring under their billowing sails, the salty gusts scrubbing their cheeks, sailors feel *they* are the true mariners. They are powering their crafts in the time-honored way and are in communion with the wind and the sea.

And yacht owners? Well, why get involved in petty rivalry? They could buy them both out.

Don't even try to use a boat owner's special language. Nautical terminology fills entire volumes. It was once useful, one supposes, to have fifty different terms for wind directions and conditions. And very disparate words for left (*port*) and right (*starboard*) to slice through life-threatening wind gusts. But why do today's boat owners seek excuses to use these esoteric nautical terms instead of our perfectly functional language?

One can only assume it's because BoatSpeak is a constant reminder to themselves, and everyone in hearing distance, that they are part of the boating elite.

The following questions, sans esoteric seafaring jargon, have been carefully constructed to help nautical illiterates launch serviceable conversation with any boat owner.

44

ICEBREAKERS

What Kind of Boat Do You Have?
The obvious preliminary and obligatory opener. If you don't hear a number in the answer, you must add, "How big is *she?*"

Then if you don't hear the words *wood, fiberglass, steel,* or *aluminum* in the answer, ask, "What is *she* made out of?"

What's Her Home Port? or Where Do You Keep Her?
The crucial word here is *her.* It separates the seafarers from the landlubbers.

Let the owner take the lead on whether the craft is called a *boat* or a *yacht.* It's a matter of size and sleeping quarters.

Do You Take Her Out Much?
Docking is always a problem, especially for northern boat owners. Ask, "Where do you keep her in the winter?"

What's the Worst Weather You've Been in? and What's Your Farthest Trip?
You've just asked for his or her recanting of tales from the sea.

What Do You Have for Electronics?
Now you'll probably hear about *radar* or *loran,* their electronic navigational systems. The boys who love toys will tell you about their *GPS* or *global positioning system.*

You can ask owners of motor-powered boats, "What do you have for *power?*" Generally the large vessels use diesel fuel and the smaller boats use gas. If you can take it, ask them to elaborate.

Are You a Racer or a Cruiser?
This one's for sailors. The answer could be a clue to your new friend's personality as well.

Do You Fish? and Do You Water Ski?

These two questions are for powerboat owners only. Ask fishermen, "Do you *troll?*" That's trailing a baited line behind the boat.

Water-skiers usually ask, "Can you *ski on one?*" and "And can you *get up on one?*" If your new friend answers yes, be sure to ask about any other "*tricks skiing.*" Some "*tricks skiers*" are towed by a toe-hold, ski backwards, and even do jumps and flips.

Do You Do Your Own Maintenance and Upkeep? Or Do You Let the Yard Do It?

All boats, from the dinkiest dingy to the largest superyacht, need a lot of *maintenance* and *upkeep.* Except for some macho motorboat owners, they love to complain about the hard work.

What's Your Favorite Gunkhole?

If you are not comfortable with this final touch of argot, just say *anchorage*, which is a place to go, drop anchor, and relax.

One final caution. Do not say "pleasure boating." That term went out with the tide over a decade ago. Now it's *boating.* The pleasure is implied.

Special thanks to Kenny Wooton, Senior Editor, *Yachting* magazine and John Jacobson, Staff Editor, *Motor Boating & Sailing*, New York, New York; Don Cullimore, Publisher and Editor, *The Water Skier*, publication of the American Water Ski Association, Winter Haven, Florida.

Talking With Bodybuilders

"The body says what words cannot," proclaimed Martha Graham. Well, truer words were never "danced" for bodybuilders. Not known for their powers of articulation, bodybuilders find audible groans while pumping iron less painful than making polite conversation.

However, if you are not content to sit silently in the shadow of the hulk's body and let his rippling muscles do all the talking, try the following questions.

When talking with women *weight training* enthusiasts, substitute *body sculpting* for *body building*. And avoid saying "body contouring," which insinuates that her plastic surgeon gave her the shapely muscles while she lay comatose on the operating table.

Bodybuilders work hard to achieve those intimidating biceps and beautiful buns. And pumping iron for many hours in the gym is not enough. They have a painstakingly planned *routine* and a diet consisting of tasteless dietary supplements. But hey, no pain, no gain.

ICEBREAKERS

You Have Incredible Symmetry. How Did You Achieve That?
You'll never go wrong with this warm-up. *Symmetry* means how the whole body appears—how it looks as a package.

47

Compliment any especially developed part of his or her body. Tell your new friend his *biceps, chest,* or *calves* have great *definition.* Talk about his *pectorals* (chest) and *abdominals* (stomach). Even say *pecs* and *abs* if the words roll comfortably off your labial tissue.

What's Your Routine?

This question takes his muzzle off. If you know a little more about bodybuilding than the average sedentary intellectual, throw this one out: "Do you *alternate* upper body with lower body?" Translation: "Do you work one day on your upper body, and the next on your lower body?"

What Kind of a Warm-up Do You Do?

No knowledgeable athlete comes near exercise equipment without an aerobic and stretching warm-up routine.

Do You Prefer Free Weights or Machines?

Iron-pumpers have strong preferences for either old-fashioned barbells or the newer Nautilus and Universal machines. If you ask him why he prefers one or the other, it promotes the evening from multiple choice to essay questions.

What Is Your Main Goal in Working Out?

A real insider's question. He or she might tell you about weight concerns, developing particular muscles for specific uses, or building lung capacity.

Have You Ever Competed?

A safe question cum compliment. Whether he does or not, you've got a new friend and a (welcome or unwelcome) bodyguard for the night.

A final warning. If the bodybuilder looks *really* massive,

avoid all discussion of "artificial enhancements" (muscle implants) or "steroid enhancement." We're talking illegal substances here and bodybuilders find it a very touchy subject. Obviously, you want to stay on the good side of anybody that much bigger than you.

Special thanks to Bob McCann, Managing Editor, *Exercise for Men Only* and *Natural Physique* magazine; and Rona Cherry, Editor-in-Chief, *Fitness for Women*, New York, New York.

Talking With Booksellers

How many bright kids just out of school, instead of taking a job at the local McDonald's, bought into the genteel fantasy of a life constantly surrounded by beloved books? Of days filled with sharing ideas, of recommending significant life-enhancing nonfiction or perhaps a new book of fine fiction to inquisitive and grateful readers? And so they became booksellers.

The dream began rapidly to dissolve, however, as the nightmare of computerized inventories, cut-raters, and competition between colossal *chain superstores* and *independents* began to encroach upon their fantasies.

These *literati* were forced no longer to think in terms of cherished books, but to start viewing *titles* as bestsellers, remainders, promotionals, or reprints.

Adding to their plight came another blow—the utter confusion of their provider, a publishing world in flux.

Many a bookseller has good reason to wish he had bought the McDonald's franchise. But something of the old fantasy lingers, and very few switch from books to burgers.

ICEBREAKERS

Are You an Independent or a Chain?
This isn't just small talk for a *bookseller*. (Always say book*seller* when talking with a bookstore owner or manager. It's elegant understatement.) Independent bookstores begin to

50

quake on their foundations at the very mention of the growing trend toward *chain* bookstores.

Do You Have Any Special Genre That You Emphasize? or How Do You Make Your Selection?

Many independent booksellers specialize in a particular type of book, either out of love or to compete with the larger stores. There are stores that specialize in cookbooks, mystery, New Age books, sports, or whatever the passion of the bookseller happens to be.

Do You Offer Any Other Services Besides Books? or Do You Have Any Special Events or Services in Your Store?

Music? Reading areas? Free coffee? Author signings? Children's readings? Actors dressing up like storybook characters? You name it—booksellers are coming up with it to help keep bodies in the store. Sooner or later, they figure, a body will find a book it wants to buy.

Do You Think That Technology Is Going to Make a Major Dent In Trade Books?

As we look into the future, we see many scholarly and reference works on screen rather than paper. Some booksellers fear readers will look to their laptops for a good read. Others swear people will never curl up around a good PC on the beach.

Foresighted booksellers are, understandably, interested in America's literacy problem, another good topic for discussion.

For Chain Bookstore Owners and Managers: What Input Do You Have Into the Buying or Marketing Decisions of the Head Office?

Which *titles* to buy, how to display merchandise, and what marketing events to hold are decisions usually made by the main office. The bookstores sometimes share in the decision-making process due to different regional and even community tastes.

For Independent Bookstore Owners and Managers: **How Do You See Your Store Fitting in With the Trend in Chain Superstores?**
Whoops. Go gently here. You risk treading on some very sore independent toes. Large chain stores are moving into many communities and expanding to offer the wider selection of books that only independents used to have.

Then again, he or she may divulge some enterprising and impassioned scheme. Booksellers are a determined lot, as diverse as the books they're struggling to sell.

Special thanks to Bernard Rath, Executive Director, American Booksellers Association, Tarrytown, New York; and Michael Coffey, Managing Editor, *Publishers Weekly*, New York, New York.

Talking With Bowlers

Don't be surprised if bowlers are a little nonplussed when you ask about their sport. They're not used to people being interested in their kind of life in the fast lane, so a few short questions go a long way.

Bowlers thumb has not yet attained the status in our society that tennis elbow has, but bowlers are working on it. The first step was to drop that gauche, blue-collar term, "alley." Bowlers now go to blue-blooded bowling *centers*. So how about a little respect?

ICEBREAKERS

Do You Bowl in a League?
Most avid bowlers play one night a week in a league. If they are not *league bowlers,* they will tell you they enjoy *open bowling*—individual bowling, or just going to the *bowling center* with a few friends.

Then show you're no bowling sloth by asking, "What night does your league bowl?"

What's Your Average? or What's Your High Game?
This is not like cross-examining a new acquaintance on her IQ or annual income. It is expected that you'll ask about scores. A candid lot, these bowlers.

When you hear the score, you must, of course, acknowledge it. So you'll know what your nod implies, here's the scorecard. The women's average is 130–140 and men's is 155–165, out of a possible 300. Consistently scoring 175 for men, 165 for women, will put the bowler in near-professional class.

"What's your *high game?*" is asking her best score. "*High series?*" asks her highest score, three games running.

Does Your Bowling Center Have Automatic Scorers?
Automatic scorers save bowlers' fingers from pencil rash. A testimony to the bowler's openness, automatic scorers also display everyone's score on overhead monitors.

Do You Follow the Tour? or Do You Watch the Pros?
You have just asked about the PBA, the Professional Bowlers Association tour.

Have You Ever Done Any Moonlight Bowling?
Moonlight bowling is a lively mixture of bowling and beer blast which many centers courageously sponsor on a Saturday night. Some call it *casino bowling, candlelight bowling,* or *rock-'n'-roll bowling.* The lights are dim. The pins are lit. The music is loud. The beer flows. Everybody's spirits go up and their scores go down. Even a nonbowler could dig this kind of blow-out.

Special thanks to Vince Aversano, Editor, *Bowling Digest,* Evanston, Illinois; and Mark Miller, American Bowling Congress, Greendale, Wisconsin.

Talking With Bungee Jumpers

When your new acquaintance says he gets his kicks from being a human yo-yo, resist the temptation to mumble "demented thrill-seeker" under your breath, at least until you've heard him out. Bungee jumping looks, and feels, a lot more dangerous than it actually is.

He'll be astonished at your grasp of the *bungee rush* when you ask, "What part do you like the best? The part where you think you're going to die, or the part where you realize you're going to live?" Basically, bungee jumping is six or seven rounds of sheer terror as you plummet toward the earth, followed by pure relief as you *boing* back up. No time for prayers for deliverance or for thanksgiving—it's all over in a matter of seconds.

There's not much else you need to know for meaningful bungee communication. But preserve his patience, and your prestige, by not asking, "What happens if the cords break?" Obviously, he's dead. Bungee jumpers delicately refer to this rare occurrence as *zeroing out* or, more graphically, *splatting*.

ICEBREAKERS

What Do You Jump From?
Less cumbersome than asking if he likes to jump from towers, cranes, bridges, or balloons—the four main *jump platforms* in decreasing order of popularity.

Do You Do Chest-Waist Jumps or Ankle Jumps ?

Most bungee jumpers attach harnesses around their hips and chests. Some attach the *cords* to their ankles so they can dive off the jump platform like an arching swan. By the second *boing*, as they call each bounce, the jumper resembles a piece of cooked spaghetti more than a swan.

Do You Jump New Zealand–or American-Style?

New Zealand, where the sport first became popular, uses a single rubber cord. More safety-conscious, or liability-insurance-minded, *American-style* uses three to five multiple cords.

Do You Think Bungee Outfits Should Be Licensed by the States They're In?

As close to a philosophical question as you'll want to come with a bungee jumper.

A *Bungee outfit* is not a fashion item. Jeans still reign supreme as bungee haute couture. A bungee outfit or *outfitter* is a crane, balloon, or tower bungee-jump operator.

Do You Usually Jump Renegade or Legal?

A real in-crowd type of rap. Jumping *renegade* is from an unlicensed platform. Save this question for when you're dangling from a chord, *boinging* with a bunch of *bungee maniacs*.

Special thanks to Eric Fair, bungee jumper and self-described "cosmic stud adventurer" and author of *California Thrill Sports*, Foghorn Press, San Francisco, California.

Talking With Cat Fanciers

Cat love, cat lore, and cat chronicling is already a multimillion-dollar business in this country. And so far, there's no relief in sight. We see new cat books every month. Not to mention cat calendars, cat photographs—even kitty albums to record pussy's first meow and paste up her first hairball.

For good communication with a cat fancier, you must first ask a fundamental reference question for the ensuing conversation—pussy's name. It's music to your new acquaintance's ears. Try to weave it into the dialogue whenever possible. For the sake of variety, you may substitute "he" or "she" when absolutely necessary. But never "it."

You'll find little difficulty getting a cat fancier to talk. In fact, you can take a catnap. When you awaken, he or she will still be chattering about Pussy.

ICEBREAKERS

What Kind of a Cat Do You Have? or **Is (Pussy) a Special Breed or Mixed Breed?**
If Pussy is a humble tomcat, cover the awkward silence by quickly asking, "Is (Pussy) a good *mouser?*" This is a genteel way of asking if the carnivorous domesticated mammal the owner is sheltering indulges in its natural predatory instincts.

What Is (Pussy's) Temperament Like?
Most effective when it immediately follows your inquiry on

Pussy's breed. Or you can ask, "Does (Pussy) have the typical (Pussy's breed) personality?" Each breed has its own traits. (The cat fancier will know what you are talking about even if you don't.)

What Do You Feed (Pussy)?

If you are sitting at dinner, save this question until after the main course. The most smitten cat fanciers will graphically describe each step of preparing Pussy's preferred cuisine— ground-up chicken necks sautéed with beef liver or heart, rolled oats, parsley—ad nauseam.

Do You Show (Pussy)?

If the cat fancier has described Pussy's appearance with some pride, this is a logical question. Whether Pussy is a *show cat* or not, all questions concerning her coat, her color, her pattern, her anything, will be answered in exhaustive detail.

Is (Pussy) Registered?

Ask this question only if you think the answer is yes. *Being registered* or *having his/her papers* means that one of the cat fancier's organizations has registered Pussy as a very classy cat.

Is (Pussy) Altered?

Or more precisely, "Is he *neutered?*" or "Is she *spayed?*" An affirmative answer means whatever Pussy was, Pussy isn't now.

Ask if Pussy's personality changed after the operation. However, if Pussy still has his/her genitals intact, you should ask, "Do you intend to breed (Pussy)?"

Did You Find (Pussy) in a Pet Shop or a Catterie?

Your new friend will appreciate that you know pussies are bred in *catteries*, not "cathouses."

Special thanks to Wini Keuler, Executive Director, American Cat Fanciers Association, Point Lookout, Missouri.

Talking With Chefs

We live in the decade of the chef as superstar. When you send your compliments to the chef at a "fine dining" restaurant, he or she will (after checking with the maître d' whether you and your party are anybody) come out in a tall *toque blanche* to take a bow. Then you must ooh and ahh over the creation *du jour* and regard each little stain of *blanquette de veau* on his white jacket as testimony to his genius.

Ah, the glamour of being a chef. Why else would he subject himself to long hours slaving over a hot stove? Why would he voluntarily imprison himself in a kitchen while his non–*food world* friends are relaxing at home or partying? Why else would he put himself in the stressful situation of racing the clock night after night? It's the glamour, of course.

Where is it? It must be hidden on the floor, sliding in the grease somewhere between the stove and the larder.

ICEBREAKERS

What Type of Food Do You Most Enjoy Cooking? or What Influences Are There in Your Cuisine?

This gets the chef started on his or her passion which, no matter how immersed a chef becomes in the business of running a restaurant, is probably still cooking.

Also ask, "Do you have any *ethnic influences* in your cuisine?" Most good chefs borrow ideas from the cuisine of other countries.

Did You Attend Culinary School, or Did You Apprentice?

An obvious demonstration of your profound knowledge of the *food service industry.* Although most aspiring chefs nowadays enter *culinary school,* many older ones *apprenticed.* Some chefs are *self-trained*—and a surprising number credit Mother.

Do You Get a Chance to Vary the Menu Day by Day?

Ambitious and creative chefs and *restaurateurs* like to vary their cuisine. Your new friend will appreciate your assumption that he or she is one of them. Incidentally, you gain many points when you drop the letter "n" and say *restaurateur* in the authentic French way.

Do You Pay Much Attention to the Visual Presentation?

Some chefs, French and Japanese most notably, maintain that the appearance of the food—the color, the shape, the layout on the plate—definitely affects taste.

Has the New Nutritional Awareness Affected Your Menu?

It's difficult to keep up with the health trend *du jour.* Some chefs try. Others simply mutter, *"Merde!"*

Do You Get Involved in the Business Side of the Restaurant?

Increasingly, chefs must be top business people. It's possible to become so immersed in this crucial aspect of the restaurant business that the chef winds up being an executive, not a cook. Ask for an opinion on this issue.

One cautionary conversational note. You would not be so banal as to ask an elevator operator if he gets his ups and downs. No less timeworn, trite, and tasteless is asking a chef, "Who does the cooking at home?"

Where Do You Dine When You Have the Time to Dine Out?
Not small talk to a rising star. Getting around to see what the competition is doing makes good business sense. Be sure to phrase this question in a way that shows you are aware that a chef doesn't have much time for this delicious research.

Special thanks to Steve Fernald, Director of Education and Apprenticeship, American Culinary Federation, St. Augustine, Florida; and Larry Lowndes, my brother, a great chef and owner of the Stanford Café, Stanford, New York.

Talking With Chess Players

After 31 . . . Rb2, Fischer looked at Spassky's gruesome threats of 32 . . . Qg1 or 32 . . . Rb1 and hurriedly forced a draw with 32 Qd8 Kg7 33 Nf5! gh, which produced perpetual check by way of 34 Qg5 Kf8 35 Qd8, and so on.

Such sensational reportage takes the breath away from chess players around the world.

From *International Grand Masters* to the humblest chess hustler cruising the southwest corner of New York's Washington Square Park for a game, chess enthusiasts agree with the English biologist, T. H. Huxley: "The chessboard is the world; the pieces are the phenomena of the universe; the rules of the game are what we call the Laws of Nature."

But that's an old chess nut.

ICEBREAKERS

Do You Play in Tournaments?
Tournaments sponsored by the United States Chess Federation and affiliated groups are held all over the country.

When speaking with chess players about their passion, the preferred term is *sport*, and many even elevate it to *the art* of chess. Highly preferable to "game."

Do You Have a Rating?
Ask this question if you think you are talking to a *rated* chess player. Most serious chess players hold a rating from the

U.S. Chess Federation. The rankings range from *unrated* or *class E* all the way up to *expert, master, senior master,* and *grand master.*

Do You Play With the Clock?

You are asking if he or she plays *speed* or *blitz* chess. This is a frantic mutual assault in which each player has a time limit of no more than five minutes and as little as one.

Are You a Problemist?

You have just asked whether he solves or composes chess problems in books and magazines.

Do You Play Computer Chess?

There are software programs and dedicated computers that do nothing but play chess. And there are dedicated chess players who do nothing but play chess.

Special thanks to Glenn Petersen, Editor, *Chess Life,* monthly magazine of the United States Chess Federation, New Windsor, New York.

Talking With Chiropractors

The world has not yet quite decided whether they are medical doctors, masseurs, or mechanics. The average person calls them *chiropractors*. Irreverent members of the medical establishment call them "charlatans," "bonecrackers," and worse. But the truly diplomatic person says *doctors of chiropractic.*

The criticism is frustrating for *D.C.'s* because they maintain they manipulate nature's most effective healer, the human body itself. You've made a friend indeed if you show sympathy with their professional plight with a comment like, "It must be frustrating for chiropractic doctors to have to fight the medical establishment just for the right to continue healing their patients."

You've made an even better friend if you start complaining about a sore back.

ICEBREAKERS

Are You in a Group Practice, or Are You a Solo Practitioner?
Many chiropractors, after a minimum of two years of college and ten semesters of chiropractic training, join a *group practice* before going out on their own as a *solo practitioner.*

Is Your Practice Based Solely on Adjusting, or Do You Also Employ Other Modalities?
You are hitting on *the* fiery internal feud with this question.

There is heated disagreement in *chiropractic* between the doctors of chiropractic called *mixers* and those called *straights*—both derogatory terms when snarled by the other. Mixers (who mix several *modalities* for curing a patient) disparage the straights for using only their hands to *adjust* the body. Straights (who feel they are purists) malign mixers for employing other modalities and machines. .

But they're bosom buddies when they're both condemning physicians for belittling doctors of chiropractic.

For Mixers: What Are Some of the Other Modalities You Use?

If the doctor of chiropractic mixes modalities, she will relish telling you about the benefits of acupuncture, heat or ice packs, electrical therapy, ultra sound . . .

For Straights: Do You Use Any Special Techniques in Adjusting?

It's the straight chiropractors' badge of honor that they adjust a patient with only their ten fingers.

What's Been Your Experience With Cooperation of Other Health Care Professionals?

You may be treading on very sore toes, or you may be talking with a D.C. who has had positive experiences. There has been recent movement in the more established medical community toward recognizing the role of the chiropractor. But according to the doctor of chiropractic, not nearly enough.

How Are Practice Guidelines Affecting Your Practice?

This issue is crippling some of the older chiropractors who are used to doing things their own way. They fear that sooner or later all compensation will be based on how well they adhere to the *practice guidelines*, which dictate precisely how they are supposed to do their job.

Do You Give Workshops?
Watch the smiling D.C. reach for a business card. After all, practically everybody is a potential participant in workshops for easing stress, headaches, and back pain.

Special thanks to Donald Petersen, Jr., B.S., H.C.D., Publisher and Editor, *Dynamic Chiropractic*, Huntington Beach, California.

Talking With Clergypeople

The unfathomed number of sects with their concoctions of creeds, doctrines, and tradition have even the most diplomatic heads spinning. To further complicate conversing with a clergyperson, you are confronting a mentality finely attuned to subtleties of generation and gender—not to mention ego.

So believe me, coming up with suitable questions to sidestep all brands of heavenly toes was no church picnic.

The following few, however, are safe and sensitive for Protestants, Catholics, and a variety of other sanctimonious souls. You'll notice a few minor word-substitutions for Catholic priests. Rabbis have a chapter of their own lest they feel too assimilated.

ICEBREAKERS

How Would You Like to Be Addressed?
In general (with the notable exception of Reverend Ike), it gets clerics' spiritual goats when anyone but a hillbilly calls them just plain "Reverend" followed by their last name. To further confuse lay folk, the proper preamble to avoid the ancient minister/pastor/father/reverend confusion is still uncodified in their doctrines.

A clergyman named Frederick Smith might want to be addressed as the Reverend Doctor Frederick Smith, Father Smith, Father Frederick, or, "Gosh, just call me Fred."

With Roman Catholic priests, however, *Father* is pretty safe. In fact, go ahead, drop it after every other word the way a musician does "man" or "dude." It shows respect. If he's real progressive, he'll tell you to cool it.

Do You Serve a Church? or Do You Have a Congregation?
Tricky Protestant verbs. They talk of *serving* a church but *having* a congregation. Same question, Roman Catholic–style, is "Are you a *parish priest,* Father?"

If he or she has a congregation (or parish) ask, "What is your *congregation* like?" (Catholic substitution is *parishioners*) And, "How large is it?" (Then subtract 10 to 20 percent from the figure and you'll have an accurate count.)

While on the subject of exaggerations, never ask a clergyperson about the *giving*—the pious euphemism for how much money the congregation puts in the kitty. Leave that discussion to the good old boys of the cloth when they get together and let their halos down.

What Style of Worship Do You Use?
This one is for less familiar denominations only. Last time you were on your knees with head bowed, you probably never thought of it as a *style of worship.* But in the biz, they categorize it as *evangelical, very formal, informal,* or *praise-oriented.*

What Part of Your Ministry (Vocation) Do You Enjoy Most?
Saying "your *ministry*" (Catholic substitution is *vocation*) rather than "your job" elevates a fairly common question to a level that deserves a diligent answer.

If you strike a good rapport, follow up with specific questions on *counseling* and *community outreach. Outreach* is a term meaning ways outside the church to help the community.

Do You Enjoy Preaching Sermons?
Some clergypeople thrive on public speaking, and others have knocking knees beneath their vestments.

If you're up for deep discussion, you may ask where he or she stands *theologically*. There is great variety even within the various denominations.

What Were the Circumstances of Your Call? or What Brought You to the Ministry?

Catholic substitution is "When did you know about your vocation?" They're just sensitive ways of saying, "How did you get into this line of work?" Every clergyman likes to feel he received a personal call (vocation) from the Man Upstairs. The Person Upstairs?

Special thanks to James Berkley, Editor, *Your Church* magazine, Carol Stream, Illinois; and Sara N. Lee, President, American Church Lists, Arlington, Texas.

Talking With Coin Collectors

A *numismatist's* great joy is, as he will tell you, holding history in his hand. He loves to caress the coins and see and feel the bedlam of the era pass before his eyes.

Like Donald Duck's Uncle Scrooge, who leaped, webbed feet first, into his pile of coins, most numismatists horde their collections at home for fondling purposes. But as Scrooge's feathered nephews Huey, Dewey, and Louie will quack, keeping all those valuable coins at home, why, that can make an old duck paranoid.

The profile of the coin collector is an educated, over fifty, well-to-do, white (90 percent) male (95 percent). These demographics are a source of some concern to numismatic associations. Not the "educated" or "white" part. Certainly not the "well-to-do," or even the "male" statistic. But the "over fifty" entry is troublesome. Unfortunately, numismatists can't continue their temporal hobby after they go to meet their Maker.

ICEBREAKERS

What Got You Interested in Numismatics?
For those who just cannot bear not flaunting their expert pronunciation of the word (noo-miss-*mat*-iks), this is a quite acceptable way to weave it in.

What Do You Collect?
Unless obvious from his answer, refine this question by asking, "Do you collect U.S. or worldwide?" or "Do you collect any particular countries?"

Do You Specialize in Any Particular Denominations?
Some collectors restrict their collecting, within a country or theme, to a particular denomination.

Do You Get Your Coins Certified? or What Condition Are Your Coins In?
You are not being indiscreet. You're simply asking what all collectors ask of each other. Numismatists send their coins to professional *grading services* to determine the *condition*. The gradings are from *uncirculated* or *mint condition* down to the bottom grade, which is called, incomprehensibly, *good.*

Are You a Member of a Coin Club?
The largest is the American Numismatic Association with over thirty-one thousand members.

Do You Go to Coin Shows?
Many numismatists regularly go to coin shows, where they share coin stories and buy, sell, trade, and fondle each other's coins.

Ever Have Any Experience With Counterfeit Coins?
Some unscrupulous types file off mint marks and change dates on coins.

Do You Think Coins and Other Numismatic Materials Should Be Taxed?
The argument rages on. Some states say, "Yes, it's taxing a hobby." Others say, "No, it's taxing money."

What Do You Think of Coins as Investments?
Interesting supply-and-demand question. The numbers of old coins is not getting any larger, and old collectors are passing away. But you needn't put it that way.

Special thanks to Steve Bobbitt, Director of Public Information, American Numismatic Association, Colorado Springs, Colorado; and Arlyn G. Sieber, Editor, *Coins* magazine, Iola, Wisconsin.

Talking With Collectors

What separates man from beast? Anthropologists have theorized it's language. Theologians argue religion. They're both wrong. It's the human proclivity to collect nonconsumable, nonvital, totally useless objects.

We applaud wealthy industrialists and famous actresses with a passion for Fabergé eggs or Lalique glass. Even our little collections of antiques or Hummel figurines draw oohs and ahhs from admiring friends.

But anthropologists, scratching their heads, can't fathom why human beings persist in collecting beer cans, conches, casino chips, old cigarette packs, cookie cutters, hat pins, and telegraph pole insulators. In fact, these particular doodads have big-enough fan clubs to warrant national societies, newsletters, and annual conventions.

One suspects that all collectors, like lottery ticket gamblers, harbor a secret hope that one day the world will recognize the value of their vast collection of thingamabobs. Recently a small-town waitress became a millionaire when a New York gallery spotted her classified ad seeking refrigerator magnets to add to her collection of twenty-three hundred.

In the meantime, collectors must settle for the recognition they receive from you.

ICEBREAKERS

What Do You Collect?
The one, the only, the obvious opener. Be sure to raise your eyebrows in approving awe when you hear the name of his or her collected doohickey.

How Did You Get Interested in Collecting (Thingamajigs)?
Many collectors had early experiences with the beloved object. Kids traded baseball cards. Mother wore hat pins. (Was the small-town waitress ever locked in a refrigerator?)

How Do You Display Your Collection?
Always a problem for the committed collector. Many collectors have built an extra room or two or three to exhibit the collection.

What Is Your Favorite or Most Prized (Gizmo)?
Saying the name of the cherished object is advisable whenever possible.

Do You Prefer Any Particular Period?
Beer bottles from the 1960s? Infant feeders from the fifties? Doorknobs from the forties? Cigarette packs from the thirties? Cookie cutters from the twenties?

Do You Buy (Doohickeys) Through the Mail?
You are displaying insider's knowledge when you ask about *mail purchases*. Collectors buy *antique trade papers* which describe an unbelievable variety of collectables for barter or sale.

Do You Get Involved in Trading Up or Dealing?
Trading up is trading in one of your whatchamacallits, and a little cash, for a better whatchamacallit.
   Dealing is selling some of your whatchamacallits to other

whatchamacallit collectors. Sooner or later most committed collectors find themselves in both roles.

Has Your Love of (Thingamajugfers) Gotten You Into Any Interesting Situations?
The *collecting fraternity* is forever sharing stories of people they've met or traveling they've done to find one more wonderful widgets to add to the collection.

Special thanks to Dale Graham, Publisher, *Antiques & Collecting Hobbies* magazine, Chicago, Illinois.

Talking With Computer Geeks

Otherwise accomplished, wise, and sober men and women suddenly remember an important phone call and leave the room when conversation turns to computers. It starts when some computer nerd, now called *geek*, starts speaking in tongues to an engrossed group who seemingly understand computerese.

The computerphobe, who can't digest one *bit* or *byte* of the conversation, has no recourse but to hastily leave the high-tech group in search of more familiar Ma Bell technology.

If you still think a *mouse* is a furry little fellow who loves cheese, here's some *technical support.* Use these questions when you want to be *compatible* with a computer user or a computer pro. Admittedly, it's elementary, but it will tide you over until you can change the subject to something you consider real, rather than *artificial intelligence.*

At which time the geek will suddenly remember an important phone call.

ICEBREAKERS

What Are You Using Your Computer For?
Sounds simple enough, but this query is right on target. He or she may be using a computer for *games, data bases, spread sheets, word processing,* or *personal information management.* These last, called *PIMs,* tell the geek when to get up, when

to go to bed, and when to schedule practically all other important mind and body functions.

Do You Have a Laptop? or What's Your Favorite Laptop?

Most computer *users* have a pet *laptop.* They love to hold the adorable little *miniframe* and stroke it. Some of them are as powerful as the walloping old institutional *mainframes* or the archaic *big boxes.*

Do You Use Any Graphics? and Do You Have Windows?

Safe questions to ask most users. The first means, "Do you make any designs, graphs, or pretty pictures with your computer?" Then ask, "What are the *graphics* for?"

The *windows* question asks if he or she is using a new system of selecting pictures off a screen that avoids the complicated commands of older computers.

Do You Belong to Any of the Computer Networks?

In addition to retrieving information, lonely computer users communicate on million-plus-member computer networks like Prodigy and CompuServe. Users have *online* conversations, and keyboard Casanovas even find electronic love. Ask what your new friend uses the network for.

For Computer Professionals: Are You Into the Hardware or Software End?

You are simply asking if he or she works with the physical aspect of computers (*hardware*) or deals with *programs* or *data (software).*

For Computer Hardware Professionals: Do You Repair Computers, or Design Components?

Repair is obvious. *Designing components* is making parts that go in computers.

For Computer Software Professionals: Do You Write Programs, or Configure Applications?

You are asking if the software person actually writes the hieroglyphiclike codes or adapts existing programs for other uses.

A must-ask for the *applications* person is, "What kinds of applications have you worked on?" This means, simply, "What have you done?"

Do You Think There Will Ever Be Compatible Open Systems?

Translation: "Do you think all the computer companies will start cooperating so their software programs will be compatible with each other?" Pose this question to both the computer pro and the computer user.

What Do You Think Is on the Horizon for Computer Use?

Be careful. You're inviting him to regale you with his *virtual sex* fantasies and more. Things are changing faster than a speeding cursor on a computer screen. Like it or not, computer technology is radically changing our world.

But that's about as far as a *computer illiterate* dare go before the discussion *crashes*. Now you're permitted to run a *search and replace* on the topic of conversation.

Special thanks to Joel Dreyfuss, Editor, *PC Magazine*, New York, New York.

Talking With Cosmetic Surgeons

Most cosmetic surgeons have a taste for both the aesthetic and pecuniary rewards of the profession. In fact, they incorporate the word into their preferred title—"aesthetic," not "pecuniary."

Aesthetic plastic surgeons, their preferred term, consider themselves to be a fairly creative lot. They talk of "restoring form, function, and beauty," and many of them are patrons of the arts, as well as patrons of the most expensive vacation packages.

Resist the temptation to ask an aesthetic plastic surgeon who some of his clients have been. You may be dying to know which starlet's second chin or politician's jowls rest in his ashcan. But it is as indiscreet to solicit this information as it is to ask a nephrologist which celebrity's kidneys are in his trophy case.

ICEBREAKERS

Do You Concentrate Your Practice More on Cosmetic or Reconstructive?

An aesthetic plastic surgeon's practice usually has greater concentration on one or the other. *Reconstructive* surgery corrects birth defects or restores facial and body structure after an accident.

If the practice is primarily reconstructive, ask about some of his or her more interesting cases. Reconstructive surgeons enjoy sharing poignant stories about people who were restored to normal life after suffering horrible accidents. Never, of course, ask the identities of the patients.

Do You Do Mostly Facial Procedures or Body Contouring?

Rhytidectomy (face lift), *blepharoplasty* (eyelid surgery), and *rhinoplasty* (nose job) are common *facial procedures.* More common *body contouring* procedures are *liposuction,* tummy tucks, and breast anything—lifting, reducing, enlarging.

How Do You Determine if Someone Is a Good Candidate for Elective Surgery? or Do You Feel That Many Patients Have Unrealistic Expectations?

How sensitive of you to know about this difficult aspect of the profession. Cosmetic surgeons encounter lots of unrealistic expectations and other bats in their patients' belfries.

Do You Have a Special Inspiration for Facial Sculpting?

Many cosmetic surgeons sculpt or paint as a hobby. Whether your new friend does or not, it's a compliment to ask, "Do you sculpt or paint?"

Do You Find It Very Different Working on Ethnic Minorities?

The artistic side of a cosmetic surgeon's nature is brought into play while, for example, shaping the nose of an Asian, an African, or native American.

How Crucial Is It That an Aesthetic Plastic Surgeon Be Board-Certified?

A much more sensitive question than the flat-footed, "Are you board-certified?"

Being *board-certified* is becoming increasingly important to them as the public becomes more aware of professional standards. The American Board of Plastic Surgery (ABPS) is the only board supported by the American Medical Association which is certified to certify aesthetic plastic surgeons. But enough about the job. Let him forget, momentarily, about the blood, the batty patients, and the lawsuits. Watch his eyes light up when you ask about his last vacation. Cosmetic surgeons are a travel agent's dream because they flock in droves to the Alps to go glacier trekking or to Africa for safaris.

Special thanks to Bob Stanton, Executive Director, and Elizabeth Sadati, PR, American Society for Aesthetic Plastic Surgery, Long Beach, California; and Laura Kopulos, Media Relations Manager, American Society of Plastic and Reconstructive Surgeons, Arlington Heights, Illinois.

Talking With Cowboys

If a rugged-looking chap with a neckerchief, a tanned chin, and a white forehead says howdy to you, you can bet he's a cowboy.

What's a greenhorn to do? Well, don't launch progressive discussions on East Coast favorites like abortion rights, feminists, the men's movement, or anything about racial problems. In fact, if you're black, he'll slap you on the back and call you "nigger"—and expect you to return the compliment by calling him a "honky muh-fuh."

Even a question like "What do you like most about your job?" is too psychobabble for these guys.

Being a cowboy is a state of mind. Cowboys ride 'em and rope 'em. They're salty, practical, and down to earth. They're independent and hate regulation of any kind. In the old days they'd tell you, "All you need to be a cowboy is guts and a horse. And if you have enough guts, you can steal a horse."

ICEBREAKERS

Where Have You Cowboyed Most?
Yes, *to cowboy* is a verb.

Is It Gettin' Harder to Keep on Cowboyin'?
You bet! Some ranchers are using motorcycles and helicopters to do a cowboy's job of roping cattle. Most cowboys can find other jobs that pay a lot better, but love keeps them in the saddle.

Do You Think the Ranching Industry Is in Trouble?
Yep. This is the hottest topic in cowboy country. Let him sound off on how all the "environmentalist wackos are making it tougher."

Do You Think You Might Be Able to Get Your Own Ranch Someday?
A cowboy's dream. Practically every cowboy wants to "run some cows of his own."

Do You Rodeo Any?
Another new verb: *to rodeo.* Some cowboys just do *ranch work.* Others are showmen who just *rodeo.* Some do both.

Have You Been to Any Cowboy Poetry Gatherings?
You're kidding. Real men don't write poetry.

Tell that to the ten thousand cowboys who show up every year in Elko, Nevada, at the *Cowboy Poetry Gathering* to recite their love of nature and their work.

Hell, ridin' a horse, writin' a verse, life could be worse.

Special thanks to Darrell Arnold, Publisher and Editor of *Cowboy Magazine,* LaVeta, Colorado; and Montie Montana, Jr., President, Buffalo Bill's Wild West Show, International Western Events, Springville, California

Talking With Crossword Puzzle Enthusiasts

Clambering around the orthographic jungle gym, adult children become addicted to crossword puzzles. You see their bodies slumped over a puzzle in an armchair. But the search for the right word is taking them around the world and through the ages. Their minds are doing battle with historians, philosophers, physicians, poets, and punsters. They are second-guessing geographers and generals—armed only with a good dictionary, a small pencil, and a big eraser.

Crossword puzzle fanatics may be able to weave intricate word tapestries where animals intersect with minerals and obscure actresses cross czars and dictators. But alas, such wordsmanship does not construct good conversation.

That's up to you. But even if you are not a disciple of across and down, you can be a *master constructor* of dialogue with these questions.

ICEBREAKERS

What Books Do You Work On?
The insider's way of asking what puzzles he or she likes to do. If the answer is the *National Review* or the *National Observer*, give a well-deserved nod of admiration. If he says the *New York Times*, amplify it with an additional nod accom-

panied by a little gasp of awe. The *Times* is considered to be one of the most difficult.

Ask what day's puzzle they like to work on. Monday is easy. It works up to almost impossible Saturday, and Sunday is potluck.

Do You Use Reference Books?
That's cheating to some purists.

Do You Have a Favorite Constructor?
Puzzles are not simply written. They are constructed by *constructors* with varying styles. As avid readers have favorite authors, crossword puzzle enthusiasts have favorite constructors.

Do You Have a Preferred Type of Puzzle?
For the buff who works on the puzzle magazines. You may hear names like *cryptic crossword, word arithmetic,* or *alphabet maze.* Ask how his or her preferred puzzles are constructed.

What Level of Problem Solver Would You Say You Are?
It's surprising that dedicated word lovers choose such banal descriptions: *easy, medium, hard, expert,* or *challenger.*

Do You Enter Crossword Puzzle Contests?
For the mainliner.

Have You Ever Tried Your Hand at Constructing Any Puzzles?
Either way, a compliment.

Do You Do Them in Pencil or Ink?
Kind of revealing, isn't it?

Special thanks to John Samson, *New York Times* Puzzle Constructor and Simon and Schuster Crossword Puzzle Editor, New York, New York.

Talking With Cruise Ship Personnel

The floating disco/hotel/restaurant/bars crowding our seaways are becoming a way of life for older middle-class American tourists. If you're a passenger, sooner or later you'll find yourself talking with a character out of *The Loveboat*.

Perhaps it's an officer who's descending from his mysterious quarters that only pretty young women are permitted to see after 10 P.M. Or a cruise staffer attempting to hide between organizing the poolside wet T-shirt contest and the beer-guzzling competitions.

You may be enjoying yourself, but it's not all fun and games for the ship's personnel. Don't make the cruise director answer the same ridiculous question one more time, "Do you sleep on the boat?" Don't ask the captain, "Gee, Captain, if you're here talking to me, who's driving the boat?" And above all, don't say "boat." It's a *ship*.

Ask, instead, these few questions about their personal lives. The *on-board personnel* will find it a welcome relief from the polyester pants and blue rinse crowd's usual chatter.

ICEBREAKERS

For the Captain: **When Did You First Become a Master?** and **What Was Your First Command?**
It's a rare passenger who knows that practically all *deck officers* have their *captain's licenses* and that only *the* captain is called

master. Becoming a master for the first time is the highlight of a seaman's life. He will relish telling you about his first *command.*

For Ship's Officers: Where Did You Attend Merchant Marine Academy?

Ship's officers work either on the *bridge* in the *deck department* or in the *engine room* in the *engine department*. It's a rare treat for a deck or engine officer to be asked about his *merchant marine academy* days.

For Cruise Staffers: Did You Come From an Entertainment Background?

Many *cruise directors* and *social hosts/hostesses* come from the performing arts. Even if the cruise staffer you are talking to didn't, he or she will appreciate the implied compliment.

They will appreciate your compliment even more in the *on-board comments questionnaire*. Many cruise lines hire, fire, and promote based on these subjective depositions.

For On-board Entertainers: How Much of the Year Do You Work Ships?

Most ship's performers divide their work year between theaters or clubs and ships. Some *work ships* year-round.

A real insider's question is "Are you booked through an agent, or do you work directly for the cruise line?"

Entertainers who are booked through an agent will enjoy telling you about other ships they have worked.

For Waiters and Cabin Stewards: Where's Home to You? Tell Me About Your Family. When Is Your Next Vacation?

Many foreign born *waiters* and *cabin stewards* are working on ships to support families in their various homelands. Perennially homesick shipboard personnel love to answer these types of questions.

The only thing they love more is getting a big tip.

Special thanks to John Godsman, President, Cruise Line International Association, New York, New York; and Captain Giorgio Accornero, Genoa, Italy.

Talking With Dancers

Wanted: Talented and attractive young men and women. Train for minimum ten years, unpaid. Must be able to withstand constant pain, spartan diet, demanding audiences, and be willing to grovel before producers. Early retirement mandatory, no pension. Competition high. Low or no pay for most engagements. Only candidates with second job as main source of support need apply.

No sane person would answer this ad. Nor would any level-headed businessperson base a career on the same capricious underpinnings that a dancer does—his or her own two tootsies. One twisted ankle and the whole operation shuts down.

So what's the payoff? Dancers are doing what they love. And how many of us can say that?

ICEBREAKERS

What Kinds of Dancing Do You Do?
The overture. Ballet? Jazz? Tap?

Are You Performing Now?
The sensitive way to ask if he or she is working. If not, ask, "What are you *working on* now?" Add, "Are you *taking classes?*" and, for a longer answer, "What are you getting out of them?"

Are You in a Company?

Professional dancers are either free-lance performers or they are employed by a *dance company*, which performs various works of one or more choreographers *in repertory.*

When Is Your Season? and What Are You Performing This Season?

Questions for the company dancer.

Have You Had the Opportunity to Do Any Work as a Soloist or a Principal?

You may gingerly ask this if she is with a company. A *soloist* dances alone and a *principal* has a starring role. The supporting performers or chorus in the *dance world* are called the *corps.*

Do You Get Most of Your Work Through Auditions or Recommendations?

A question for the independent dancer. Like professional actors and actresses, many dancers *audition* for musicals, dance revues, or nightclub shows. Others, in the relatively small world of professional dance, get their *roles* or *bookings* by *recommendation.*

Whose Choreography Do You Prefer?

Venture this only if you know something about the work of various choreographers and can keep up with the dancer's impassioned response.

Many dancers love to choreograph their own work. Ask, "Have you done any choreography? Tell me about it."

Special thanks to Richard Philp, Editor-in-Chief, *Dance Magazine,* New York, New York; and Rickey Geiger, Executive Secretary, National Dance Council of America, and President, North American Dance Teachers Association, Vienna, Virginia.

Talking With Dentists

Very few single words in the English language conjure up as much pain, aggravation, and disagreeable expense as *dentist.* Sadly, no one but hopeful mothers of the bride express any warm sentiments about dentists.

And yet, as a group, they're really terribly decent folks, and are, while working at least, wonderful conversationalists.

There is no end to the essay questions dentists ask while hovering over your gaping orifice. What finely tuned ears they must have to understand your garbled answer, and then diplomatically continue as though you had said something cogent. By the time you've gargled, expectorated, and prepared to elaborate on your response, the wizard is on to yet another subject.

Whether they are as conversationally accomplished when you have all of your speech organs unencumbered, however, varies from dentist to dentist. But these questions should get even the most laconic to open wide and talk with you.

ICEBREAKERS

Are You in General Practice, or Do You Have a Specialty?
If he or she has a general practice, ask, "What *phase* of dentistry do you enjoy the most?"

Do You Have Associates or Do You Practice Alone?

Your rare appreciation of the high cost of dental equipment inspires this question.

Ask also, "Are you affiliated with any of the hospitals?" Dentists often do *pro bono* work at the local hospitals.

How Are You Coping With the OSHA and EPA Regulations?

A question of vital importance to today's dentist. They like to grouse about how the Occupational Safety and Health Act and the Environmental Protection Agency are complicating their lives through "excessive" paperwork, precautions, and regulations. Dentists must pay for these practices out of pocket, and noncompliance results in fines.

Are You Finding Yourself Talking to Your Patients' Physicians More?

The trend in medicine is toward *whole body issues*, and dentists are striving for greater communication among medical disciplines.

Do You Find Your Practice Patterns Changing With an Older Population?

The simple filling 'n' drilling days are disappearing. Because older patients want to retain their teeth longer, more dentists are drawn into oral medicine.

Do You Do Any Lecturing or Writing on Your Specialty?

A good question for the specialist. Dentists, in a profession that is perceived to be totally lacking in glamour, have few outlets for expressing their creativity other than the sculptures they create in your mouth. Lecturing and writing are two ways they gain recognition, at least among their peers.

How Do You Feel About Professional Advertising?

Some dentists, especially the older ones, consider advertising to be in bad taste. Ask his or her opinion.

Publicity is another interesting conversational avenue to explore. Even some dentists who are skeptical about advertising retain publicists to help get their names out to the public.

Are You Tired of the Pain Jokes?
Yes.

Special thanks to Judy Jukush, Editor, *American Dental Association News,* Chicago, Illinois

Talking With People With Disabilities

When talking to a person who has a disability, there's one important secret to good rapport. If only it were so simple with ABs—short for *able bodies*, what they call us. Adjust one tiny screw in your head: think *people* first, *disability* second.

After that minor brain tune-up, even our language changes. You'll be saying *person with a disability*, not "handicapped person." You'll say *visually impaired*, not "blind," and *hearing impaired*, not "deaf." You'll talk about someone *in a wheelchair*, not a "wheelchair-bound" person. And when you speak the new language, you'll feel their gratitude.

Topics to discuss? Anything, because people with a disability carry the same baggage through life as everyone else. They just lug one extra piece.

Should we ignore their disabilities? No, it's obvious to them that it's obvious to us. But let them take the lead.

The following questions are for when your new friend seems ready to talk about his or her *physical challenge*.

ICEBREAKERS

What Do You Have in Your Home as Special Accommodations?
Everyone with a disability has made accommodations. You may hear about some pretty ingenious ones.

93

How Does Your Company Work With the Accessibility Problem?

This question is, of course, aimed at someone who is in a wheelchair. Ask about other accommodations for other disabilities.

How Did You Come Upon Your Disability? or Have You Had Your Disability Since Birth?

This treats the disability as something that he wears or has, not as an integral part of him. Avoid the word "handicapped."

Were You a (Name of Profession) Before Your Accident (Disease)?

A question for a person whose disability is more recently *acquired.*

Did Your (Talent, Profession) Develop Further After the Accident (Disease), or Is It a Bigger Challenge Now?

This shows that you do not think of your new friend as a victim but as someone who is functioning with a physical challenge. And as with any challenge, dealing with a disability may push a person to advance a skill or talent.

Special thanks to Patricia Johnson, Editor, *A Positive Approach*, Melville, New Jersey; and Tammy Davidson, Director of Education, Adventures in Movement for the Handicapped, Dayton, Ohio.

Talking With Doctors

The tremendous prestige accorded physicians is a perplexing phenomenon. As a friend, a little too close to the profession to sustain the usual reverence, asked, "Why is it that we put somebody up on a pedestal who sticks his fingers into all of our orifices and looks at our stool?"

The answer is, of course, monetary. You can recognize a prestigious doctor, like a fashionable pelican, by the size of his bill. And everyone knows, "God heals while the doctor takes the fees."

Pity the poor physician. Man and the press have not been kind to him. But for as long as man is likely to die and yet desires to live, doctors will be made fun of—and very well paid.

In order to combat the constant assault by the press and eternal ridicule by an envious public, physicians have worked on developing a strong and healthy ego. Most have been quite successful.

For good rapport with a physician, ask one or two short questions to demonstrate your keen perception of the medical milieu, and then move on to something else.

Doctors' preferred topics are their leisure activities (of which they can afford the best) and their wonderful business acumen (of which they have none). Their least favorite subject is medicine.

Unless they're powwowing in private with their accomplices, trying to save your life.

ICEBREAKERS

What's Your Specialty?

The obvious conversational kick-starter. Drive it off with "What drew you to that *specialty?*" (The *specialist* is, obviously, the doctor with a smaller practice and a bigger boat.)

You may also ask, "Are there any new medical advances on the horizon in your specialty?" Long before we hear anything about new studies and research, physicians read about them in the medical journals. Also, if there's a current issue in the news impacting on his or her specialty, ask for an opinion.

Do You Think There's Too Much Subspecialization Going On?

As the field of medicine evolves, more *subspecialties* are becoming certifiable. Both the specialist and the almost extinct species of general practitioner are sure to have an opinion.

Are You Affiliated With a Hospital? or How's Your Relationship With Your Hospital?

A very relevant question because, as hospitals become increasingly more commercial, their relationship with the physician changes. He or she often gets the short end of the stick.

Is This What You Bargained For? or Does Medicine Look Different Today Than It Did Twenty Years Ago?

The first question is for young doctors, the second for older *docs.*

Young people who entered medical school less than a decade ago went in with very different expectations. There have been many recent changes in medicine due to government regulations, insurance costs, and a host of other factors.

Incidentally, *docs* is an insider's word which implies a level of familiarity that you don't have unless you've been hanging out with docs all your life. Stick with *physician*. They like being distinguished from Ph.D.'s, optometrists, veterinarians, chiropractors, and all mail-order "doctors."

With Health Care Reform Coming Down the Pike, Is Medicine Going to Be the Way You Would Want It to Be?
Gets the physician speculating on the future. Various health care issues facing the country, such as *national health insurance* and the *uninsured*, have the ability to get him in two places where it hurts simultaneously—his conscience and his pocket.

How Is the Current Medical Environment Affecting You?
Personalizes it. The walloping number of regulations, practice guidelines, and the high *cost of practice* give all doctors a lot of grief, especially the private physician.

The more philosophical physicians appreciate invitations to talk about life-and-death matters such as living wills, euthanasia, extending the life of terminally ill patients, and their malpractice insurance carrier.

But now it's time to move on to other subjects. Cars, books, boats, trips, investments, leisure activities. A physician never tires of discussing these vital issues.

Special thanks to Paul Tarini, Senior Public Information Officer, American Medical Association, Chicago, Illinois.

Talking With Dog Owners

In the interest of equal time with cats, I offer this chapter. Most dog owners, however, with the promiscuous exception of the French, are less effusive about their pet love.

Reticence notwithstanding, the bonds of love between a human and dog are no less powerful. We are a nation brought up on dog lore. The heroic Rin-Tin-Tin, the legendary Lassie, and Dorothy's Toto in *The Wizard of Oz* are a more likable lot by far than Alice's Cheshire Cat or the flea-infested Sylvester, who rummages through trash cans.

Cat fanciers accuse man's best friends of being obsequious and slavish bone polishers. But dog lovers will not be swayed. They respond, "Do you prefer a pet who jumps on your lap out of affection—or one who makes the leap merely because your lap is warmer than the floor?"

ICEBREAKERS

What Breed Is Your Dog?

Always the first question, followed closely by asking the dog's name. You will, of course, avoid the impersonal "he" or "she," or the inadmissible "it," when talking about your new friend's four-legged family member.

Why Did You Get This Breed? and What Is a (Name of Breed) Like to Live With?

This shows you know that life with a Pekingese is not quite like coexistence with a Saint Bernard.

98

Then ask, "Is (Flossie) a typical (name of breed)?" If she's a mutt, skip the breed question, and ask, "What kind of personality does (Flossie) have?"

What Activities Do You Engage in With (Flossie)?
Running, driving, eating, sleeping, following her around the block with a pooper-scooper?

Does (Flossie) Know Any Commands or Tricks?
With this question you are asking if the pooch has any training in *commands* like "sit," "stay," or "heel."

On the other paw, *tricks* are outstanding skills like lying down, rolling over, and playing dead.

What Training Techniques Do You Employ?
The most common *training technique* is giving pooch a *treat* or *food reinforcement* when he responds to the right command. Accompanying rewards are praise, friendly pats, big smiles combined with "Goooood dog!" and other expressions of the human's astonished approval.

Do You Show Your Dog?
Ask only if you suspect that Flossie is a classy canine. *Purebred* dogs have registration papers to show they're really *pedigreed pups*.

Do You Show in Conformation or Obedience?
Showing *in conformation* is matching the dog up with the standards for that breed in appearance and temperament. Showing *in obedience* is demonstrating the dog's ability to obey commands.

Ask what *shows* and *competitions* Flossie's been in and what ribbons she's won.

Do You Breed Your Dog(s)?
Now we're talking doggie business. The *dog breeder* may sell

blue-blooded tail waggers to pet shops, other breeders, or individuals who want pups with papers.

Do You Breed Show Dogs?

Folks who breed *show dogs* feel they are the highest echelon of dogdom. With the usual well-bred flair for understatement, these professionals call themselves *hobby breeders*. That distinguishes them from what they disparagingly call the *backyard breeder*, whose little Flossie simply has puppies.

Special thanks to Kim Thornton, Editor-in-Chief, *Dog Fancy* magazine, Mission Viejo, California; and Donna Marcel, Editor, *Dog World*, Chicago, Illinois

Talking With (Print) Editors

You never heard a kid say, "Hey, when I grow up, I wanna be an *editor!*" It's because most editors are writers at heart. But they are writers who like to eat. So they become editors.

What does an editor do? He or she goes to work in the morning to a publishing house, newspaper, or magazine, and then passes the day, well into the evening, saying no to most writers and yes to all more senior editors. The remaining time is spent reading with scissors.

The pay for this chore of separating the wheat from the chaff (and then printing the chaff, accused Adlai Stevenson) is low. The hours are long. The hassles are high. And the politics are detestable to their refined artistic temperaments.

So where's the satisfaction? Perhaps it's the joy of finding a beautiful piece of writing—and then simplifying it. Or the satisfaction of being able to use the editorial *we*, at least in private, when an article, book, or story is well received. (Even Mark Twain acknowledged that only editors and people with tapeworms have the right to use the editorial *we.*)

Be compassionate to your new friend. Editors are drawn and quartered daily by finicky bosses, fickle advertisers, fluctuating egos, and flaky writers.

ICEBREAKERS

What's Your Publication?
EditorSpeak for "What magazine or newspaper do you work

at?" (For book editors, see publishing chapter. For more on newspaper editors, see the chapter on newspaper journalists). Ask how often the publication is *put out.* Monthly? Weekly?

If he or she is simply introduced as an "editor," it is appropriate to ask "What *kind* of an editor are you?" Your new acquaintance might say *executive editor, managing editor* or the hands-on *production editor.* An *acquisitions editor* acquires material for the publication, and a *copy editor* thoroughly reads and grammatically corrects manuscripts. Many editors bear one title but wear lots of hats.

Who Are Your Readers?
A demographic question for editors of major publications or of specialty magazines like, say, one aimed only at dancing doctors in the Northeast.

If you've never heard of the publication, disguise your ignorance of their magazine's anonymity by asking, "Could I pick up a copy of *(Northeast Dancing Doctors)* on the news stand?"

What's Your Circulation?
A numbers question. You're asking what's the largest number of readers they can brag to advertisers about. Ask for a breakdown. "How much of that is *newsstand sales* and how much is *subscription?*"

Did You Come to (Name of Publication) Through a Background in Journalism or in (Publication's Subject Matter)?
Example, "Did you come to *Northeast Dancing Doctors* from a background in journalism, or were you a waltzing physician from Vermont?"

Ask how long he or she has been with the magazine or paper, or "Have you been with the publication since its *launch?*" *Launch* is the term for the publication's inception.

Don't panic for the editor when you hear him talk about

the closing. *Closings* are the normal, preplanned panic days when each *issue* is *put to bed*, or made ready for printing.

Editors who *are* talking devastation use the gentle euphemism, *folding*.

Is the Job What You Expected It to Be?

An insightful query especially for journalism—*J-school*—graduates. They started out as word people and now must concern themselves with numbers.

Other personal questions they might enjoy are "Do you do any writing?" and "Do you get out on the road much?"

Are Your Articles Mostly Staff Written or Do You Use Free-Lancers?

You are asking if the editorial staff of the magazine or newspaper write most of the articles, or *copy*, or whether they hire outside writers.

Is Your Advertising Up?

Go gently here. Essentially you are asking how the paper or *book* (insider's word for "magazine") is doing. Magazine editors talk in terms of *advertising pages.*

How's Your Relationship With Your Publisher?

A variation on the old "Do you like your boss?" question. Just one of the problems for an editor is publishers who encourage editorial support for advertisers—articles that promote the interests of a product or service.

How Do You Stay on Top of What Your Readers Want?

An open-ended question that may bring elaborate answers about highly paid research organizations or dime store crystal balls.

Special thanks to Marlene Kahan, Executive Director, American Society of Magazine Editors, and Mark Clements, President, Mark Clements Research, New York, New York.

Talking With Engineers

Engineering schools don't prepare graduates for what they are *really* going to find on the job. The technical training is fine. But they ill equip earnest young engineers for the inevitable institutional politics, the backstabbing, and all the bottom-of-the-double-boiler bosses—the ones who shoot off a lot of steam but never really know what's cooking.

Talking with an engineer can be tricky. Slithering inside of greasy turbines is their kind of fun, not making polite conversation at dinner parties. Engineers are problem solvers and troubleshooters, not gabbers. Just ask one and he'll nod his head in agreement.

The various fields of engineering are countless and complex. But here are a few sharp ice picks to get any engineer talking. Until something breaks at the party and he rushes off to fix it.

ICEBREAKERS

What Kind of an Engineer Are You? or What Field of Engineering Are You In?
Just for openers. Mechanical? Civil? Chemical? Electrical? How about astrophysical?

What's Your Specialty Within Your Field?
Starts to narrow it down.

A vocabulary note before proceeding. With an engineer,

use tough macho words like *plant, facility,* and *site.* Avoid sissy words like "company" or "location."

Do You Work in Industry or for a Firm?

Or possibly in academia? If you are talking with a *consulting engineer* or one in private practice, ask about the clients.

What Project Are You Involved in Now?

Project is the key word here. This is the most effective question a layman can ask to get an engineer talking. He or she will reward genuine curiosity with an answer at least a couple of sentences long.

Do You Think We Have Sufficient Engineering Skills to Retain Our Competitive Edge?

Now you're graduating from small talk into one of the industry's major concerns. Already engineering science is losing out in research and development (and in producing things that don't fall apart) to the usual tough competitors in the Pacific Rim and Germany. Ask for his or her theories on why.

How Would (Name of Specialty) Impact on My Daily Life?

To bring him back in for a landing.

Special thanks to Dr. Woodrow Leake, Deputy Executive Director, American Society for Engineering Education, Washington, D.C.; and Larry Beck, Editor-in-Chief, *Engineer's Digest,* Overland Park, Kansas.

Talking With
Environmentalists

"It's not that easy bein' green," croaked Kermit the Frog. Not to deter environmentalists, however. The challenge comes with the commitment.

For starters, establishing good rapport with environmentalists demands a precise vocabulary and no smoking. It's no small task speaking with a green tongue, when the terms are continually evolving. Even the word *environmentalist* is becoming polluted. It has been snarled too many times through clenched teeth by those acrimoniously accused of favoring fishermen over fish and industry over turtles.

At this writing, however, it is still safe to let *environmentally aware* pass from your lips as you ask the following questions in GreenSpeak.

ICEBREAKERS

What Are the Biggest Current Threats to Our Environment?
Gets the *environmentally aware* person to focus on the particular niche of the environment that most concerns him or her.

Are You Involved in Any Community Actions?
Actions and *activists* are very green words. If you ask, "Do most of the people in your community feel the way you do?"

he or she will tell you whether the battle is a lonely one or a community bash.

Do You Think Real Change Happens at a Grass-Roots Level or at the Governmental Level?
A good probe, especially for the community activist.

Do You Get Any Government Support for Your Actions?
Open this door only if you are ready to talk politics.

Do You Think We Should Try to Work Globally or Just Take Care of Our Immediate Biological Resources?
The green people fall into two camps on this one. Some feel we should, and can, only take care of our own forests and wildlife. Others feel we must be more *globally aware.*

Do You Think It's Possible to Make Legislation for Other Ecosystems That We're Not Familiar With?
Now you have asked the question that keeps environmental philosophers awake at night.

If you are going to learn just one new green word, let it be *ecosystem.* Hardly anybody knows precisely what it means, but it's bandied about at every green gathering. (Best definition I've heard so far is "all interactions of a community of organisms with each other and with the physical environment.")

This question is like asking if inner-city jungle inhabitants should try to make legislation for African jungle inhabitants. Or if Capitol Hill dwellers should concern themselves with Appalachian foothill dwellers.

Special thanks to Mark Cherrington, Editor, *Earthwatch Magazine*, Watertown, Massachusetts.

Talking With Farmers

The image of the farmer as a hayseed in bib overalls went out with the old horse-drawn plow. The young farmer today may know how to adjust a corn planter and get milk out of a cow, but if he's not a savvy businessman, he's going to be swallowed by the corporate thrashing machine.

Traveling salesmen, forget all the farmer's daughter jokes you ever heard. She and her mom have no time to even wink at you. They're too busy supervising in the fields or doing sophisticated crop analysis and tax records on the farm's computer.

Farmers still call it *farming,* but Washington has named it *agribusiness,* and it's getting tougher all the time. But in spite of dwindling profits, many *agriculture families* stay with it out of love.

Take Farmer Jones who just won millions in the state lottery. When asked what he's going to do with it, he replied, "Oh, I suppose I'll just keep on farming till it's all gone."

ICEBREAKERS

How's the Weather Been?
No kidding. This is quintessential small talk to city slickers, but to a farmer, it is vital. No matter how careful the farmer is, one big storm can wipe out months of work.

How Many Acres Do You Have? and **Got Any Livestock, or Are You All Crops?**
If he has *livestock*, find out what kind. Beef cattle? Dairy cattle? If it's *crops*, ask, "What's your main crop?" Nowadays, most farmers specialize.

What's the Market Outlook for (Farmer's Crop)?
Don't let the work hands and the ruddy tan fool you. The new breed of farmer can tell you about commodities and market developments worldwide.

Do You Hire Any Help, or Does the Family Do It All?
This too sounds casual. But you have asked a significant question for *agricultural families.* The farm labor situation is becoming increasingly critical. Sit back and let him share some of his woes with you.

What's Your Opinion of the GATT Talks? and **How Are They Going to Affect Your Operation?**
Every farmer has a heated opinion on the General Agreement on Tariffs and Trade.

How Are Environmental Concerns Impacting on Your Operation?
Ditto. Farmers are basically strong conservationists, but they don't want to suffer whatever nature throws at them without some chemical warfare to fight back.

Special thanks to Bernard Staller, Chief Operating Officer, National Young Farmer Educational Association, Alexandria, Virginia; and Don Tindall, Publisher and Editor, *Cooperative Farmer,* Richmond, Virginia.

Talking With Firefighters

Firefighters are those crazy fools who go running into a burning building when everybody else is running out. You know, the ones obsessed with saving the lives and property of strangers.

Firemen and firewomen are the nicest people you never want to meet, at least on the job, at your burning home. But if you run into one socially, show the firefighter that you know his or her acts of heroism are all in a day's work.

ICEBREAKERS

Are You a Professional or a Volunteer?

This question determines whether you're talking with a firefighter who lives in the firehouse a third of his life, or a volunteer who jumps out of bed or bathtub when he hears the siren. The big moment is called *responding to an alarm.* Old-timers still call it *going on a run* from the old days when the firemen actually ran after the horse and hose wagon.

You don't gain brownie points with a career professional by talking about your brother-in-law, the volunteer firefighter. The pros don't have a lot of reverence for those who, as they say, "do it as a hobby." The volunteers feel they can do the job just as well, and for free.

Are You an Officer?

The ranks, in descending order, are *fire chief, deputy or assistant chief, battalion chief, captain, lieutenant.* Below the officers are the *driver* and *firefighters* grades three and two; grade one is the entry level.

Are You With an Engine or Truck Company?

A fire *department* is divided up into *companies*. The *engine company* firefighters stretch the hose, plug it into the hydrant, and put out the fire. The *truck company* firefighters ride the truck which has a ladder, tools, and axes to break through walls. There are also *big ladder trucks*, which carry the huge extension ladders with the platform.

Do You Also Do Emergency Medical Services?

Many firefighters are trained in CPR, mouth-to-mouth resuscitation, and in administering other medical services.

What Kind of Ongoing Physical Training Do You Have?

It varies from department to department, but all firefighters undergo continual and rigorous *PT* or *physical training*.

What Kind of Turnout Gear Do You Wear?

Just knowing the term *turnout gear* merits you the long version replete with descriptions of heavy yellow fire retardant jackets, bunker pants, big boots, helmets with eye shields, and *SCBA, self-contained breathing apparatus.* A firefighter in *full turnout* is carrying about seventy pounds of equipment.

What's Life Like in the Fire House? Do You Have Many Women in Your Company? Do You Enjoy Cooking Duty? What Kind of Razzing Did You Get as a Proby?

These four questions invite tales about life in the fire *station* or *house*, which, as any firefighter will tell you, is a world unto itself. Since the relatively recent introduction of women, life has changed for the fireman, starting with pajamas. But everybody still gets cooking duty. Ask about their favorite recipes. Yes, even the men.

Don't forget to ask about the wicked razzing that *proby* or *rookie* firefighters endure.

Tell Me About Some of the Big Ones.

A *big one* is, of course, a big fire. Firefighters from all over run into each other at big fires.

When it comes time to say so long to your new friend, say, *"See ya at the big one!"* It's their insider's way of saying, "See you later, buddy."

Special thanks to George Burke, Director of Communications, International Association of Firefighters, Washington, D.C.; and Lester Tyra, Editor, *Fire Fighter*, Houston, Texas.

Talking With Fishermen

Fishing was once a simple pastime. All you needed was patience and a big worm. While dedicated *anglers* still feel fishing is almost a religious experience in which they return to the simplicity of their forefathers, today's *sport fishing* is big business. And anglers communicate with their ancestors and each other in a vocabulary that rivals that of the space program.

Mastering their language is impossible. Don't even try. Fishermen's ears, accustomed to fish stories, will easily detect your bluff. Ask instead these rudimentary questions with sincere curiosity. They will not make you piscatorially eloquent. But you'll break the ice with an angler, even if the only fish you've ever seen was filleted on your plate.

ICEBREAKERS

What Kind of Fishing Do You Do?
For experts and novices alike. The answers will be self-explanatory—*freshwater, saltwater.* Be sure to ask if he or she fishes from a boat, in a stream, or from shoreline.

Do You Fish Mainly on Weekends, or Do You Go Out on Longer Fishing Trips?
To determine just how serious he or she is about the whole thing. A natural follow-up question is, "Where's the best fishing?"

113

Have You Ever Done Any Fly Fishing?
For a fisherman, this is the highest art, akin to ballet. *Fly fishing* is flinging a floating hook, all gussied up in feathers to look like a small insect, through the air on the end of a line attached to a long flexible rod.
Casting a line into the ocean from the shore is called *surf casting.*

What Kind of Tackle Do You Use?
You are asking about all that gear he lugs to the stream or aboard his boat for better communion with his forefathers.

What Kind of Lures or Bait Do You Use?
Even if you have no idea what he's talking about, some of the names can be fun: lullybugger, bucktail, cork bug, dusty miller, Jock Scot. They're all just fancy ways to disguise a hook as a dragonfly, mouse, or some other fish treat.

Do You Belong to Any Fishing Associations? or Do You Fish in Tournaments?
Save this one for the serious sport fisherman.

What's the Biggest Fish You Ever Caught (or the Biggest One That Got Away)?
Only if you dare.

Special thanks to Michael Leech, President, International Game Fish Association, Fort Lauderdale, Florida.

Talking With Flight Attendants

Lest you haven't been commercially airborne since the *Coffee, Tea, or Me* days, there have been a few changes above the troposphere.

They start with the name. Those whose sensibilities predate women's liberation will still be tolerated saying "airline stewardess," but the aeronautically correct term is now *flight attendant.* Women still outnumber men, but today's flight attendant is likely to have a husband at home taking care of the kids while she flies off to foreign ports.

The age limitations, red lipstick, girdles, and plastic smiles that "stew schools" used to require have been flattened by the unions. Now you will be served hot coffee by a real woman—and have it dumped in your lap if you call her a "stew."

From the days when the first lovesick *stew bum* tried to master their lingo, *airline crews* have been asking each other the same questions in the same way. Here they are, for whatever purpose you might find them useful.

ICEBREAKERS

Who Do You Fly For?
This is short for "What airline do you fly for?" and even shorter for "Whom do you fly for?" But it's the unalterable

opener between *flight crews,* which include *flight attendants, pursers, pilots, copilots,* and *first officers.* These last three are the *cockpit crew.*

Do You Fly International or Domestic?
Ask this if the answer is not obvious from your knowledge of the airline's routes.

What's Your Favorite Layover?
You have just asked her which city of the airline's routes she enjoys staying overnight in the most.

Do You Bid for Routes?
The system of *assigning routes* (giving flight attendants a schedule for the month) is based on *seniority.* The most senior have first crack at the best routes or the most days off.

Two good follow-up questions are, "Are you senior enough to get the routes you want?" and "Do you bid for days off or for destinations?"

What Kind of Travel Privileges Do You Get?
The airlines offer various travel passes to in-flight personnel and their families.

How Has Airline Deregulation Affected You?
If she has been on the job since the Reagan reign, she's seen some changes and is lucky to still have a job.

Special thanks to Dee Maki, National President, Association of Flight Attendants, Washington, D.C.

Talking With Gamblers

Gambling is a costly passion for rich and poor alike. A roll of the dice can make a rich person poor and a poor person rich—for a few hours at least.

Even if you contend the best roll of the dice is to throw them away, avoid philosophical and theological discussions with a gambler. Leave the morality of his passion to his clergyman and heirs.

Besides, nothing you say will dissuade him. Gambling is legal heroin to a *high roller*. He loves the rush of blood gushing through his veins at twice the normal velocity while he maintains a calculatedly cool exterior. He's Mr. Cool in combat, taking it right where *real* men know it hurts—in the wallet.

ICEBREAKERS

What Game Do You Play?
Get this out of the way first. A little casino brief: the *vigorish* (house profits) on roulette hovers around 4 percent. Craps is down to 2 or 3 percent. And blackjack can actually be in the gambler's favor if played right.

Don't even mention the slots. The big boys go many tables out of their way to avoid being spotted in one-armed bandit lane. The *vig* is the worst on the slots, around 20 percent.

Have You Made Any Big Scores?
A more supportive question than, "Yo, how those GA (Gamblers Anonymous) meetings been goin'?"

What's Your Strategy? or Do You Have a System?

This should carry you through the rest of the evening. A *system* is a "scientific" way of wagering based on a formula rather than hunches. All systems sound absolutely fail-safe, across a dinner table.

The *handicapper* (one who studies and makes bets on horses) relies a little less on systems and hunches. He puts his money on tangible elements like performance records of horses, watching jockeys, and gauging starting positions, track conditions, purse sizes, and horses' eye color.

Do You Have Any Superstitions?

Ask with a wink. Superstitions abound, such as only going to certain windows to make bets or keeping tickets only in the left pocket—the usual.

Do You Parlay Your Bets? and Do You Set a Loss Limit for Yourself?

These are questions for the small-time, more intellectual dabbler. You are asking whether he puts his winnings back into play or sets a loss amount at which he'll quit.

Again, this is not a question for the big boys. The word *loss* might make them ill.

What Qualities Do You Think Makes a Good Gambler?

A little implied compliment never hurt anyone. And there could be advantages. If you treat the *high roller* with esteem, his hunches may make him gamble on doing business with your company. He may even go against the odds and put *telephone numbers* (big money) on you—no matter how much of a *sucker bet* you are. That's the kinda guy he is.

Special thanks to Michael Mausert, Business Manager, *Win Magazine* and *Gambling Times*, Van Nuys, California; and Barry Meadow, Author, *Money Secrets at the Racetrack*, Anaheim, California.

Talking With Gardeners

Some devoted gardeners feel almost spiritual about their hobby. They are working in harmony with the forces of nature and recreating a microcosm of life. Others garden because they don't like going to the supermarket for vegetables.

Gardeners will complain they need a cast iron back with a hinge in it. Maintaining a healthy garden is no easy task, and many an aspiring gardener has thrown in the trowel after a few attempts. If you compliment your new friend's fortitude, you'll show him or her that you're no gardenless-variety city straphanger. Then follow up with these few garden-variety questions.

ICEBREAKERS

Do You Grow Mostly Ornamentals or Vegetables?
If you feel uncomfortable with the word *ornamentals*, by all means substitute *flowers*. However the term *ornamentals* is more inclusive and obviously more impressive.

Do You Have More Annuals or Perennials?
Everyone learns (and then gets confused) that *perennials* are those plants that come up every year; *annuals* must be planted every spring.

Do You Grow From Seed or Transplant?
Impatient gardeners start poring over the seed catalogs a

months or so before the last *frost date* in their area. Since it is more difficult to grow from seeds, garden centers are crawling with neophyte gardeners seeking seedlings that have already sprouted.

Do You Have to Deal With a Lot of Shade or Pests in Your Garden?
This shows your sacred knowledge that there is no Eden. Pests are everywhere.

Shade is another challenge. Some plants, of course, thrive on shade—but usually not the ones the gardener wants to grow that year.

Have You Done Any Companion Planting?
An especially timely question while she is complaining about pests. Some plants have a symbiotic relationship and repel pests from each other. Others deposit nutrients into the soil that another plant needs. They call growing these chummy plants together *companion planting.*

How Do You Prepare Your Soil? or Do You Add Soil Amendments?
Open-ended questions to get the gardener passionately talking about *double digging, composts* from the year before, *soil tests,* ad infinitum.

For City Folks: Have You Done Any Community Gardening?
Community gardening is very popular in larger cities, where cement-sore feet long to dig their toes into the soil.

Ask whether the garden is mostly *individual plots* or *communal space,* the entire garden belonging to all. Then ask "Is your land *permanently preserved?*"—the biggest issue for community gardeners. They want their pastoral patch permanently and legally protected.

Do You Think It's Possible to Have a Completely Organic Garden?

Gardeners, since the first environmentalists' march on Washington, have put their green thumbs together in prayer asking their Maker, "If You can do it, why can't I?"

Special thanks to Kay Olson, Executive Editor, *Flower & Garden Magazine,* Kansas City, Missouri; and Tessa Huxley, President, American Community Gardening Association, Philadelphia, Pennsylvania.

Talking With Golfers

So you find yourself talking to a Sunday golfer who's out there hacking at the ball on Friday afternoons, Saturdays, Sundays, Mondays, and any other day his absence might go unnoticed at the office. And you, like most of the non-English-speaking world (except the Japanese, who are fast on their way to becoming mainliners), think, like Mark Twain, that golf is the way to ruin a perfectly good walk.

Relax and take full swing with the following questions for nongolfers. While he or she is zealously answering them, you'll have plenty of time to contemplate how to change the subject. And all before your new friend realizes you don't know the difference between a driver and a putter and could care less.

ICEBREAKERS

What's Your Handicap? or What's the Strength of Your Game?

Without exhausting noncurious nongolfers with scoring explanations, suffice it to say that if the answer is in the 120s or lower, you show appropriate awe. If you're uneasy saying *handicap*, ask "What's the strength of your game?" Or even, "How ya been hittin' 'em?" Remember, golfers need very little encouragement to talk about their game.

What Kind of Clubs (Irons, Woods, Sticks) Do You Have?
Choose from the above four words depending on the level of familiarity you want to express—and the degree to which you will understand the answer.

What Courses Do You Play? or Have You Traveled to Any Good Courses?
These safe questions serve a dual purpose. They thrill the golfer and provide you easy access into changing the subject to a lively travel discussion.

What Are Some of Your Better Shots?
This results in an unstoppable, excruciatingly slow motion, hole-by-hole replay.

Where's the U.S. Open This Year?
A respectable curiosity, because the location changes every year. But be careful not to get mixed up and ask where the *Masters* is next year. It's always in Augusta, Georgia. Ergo, your asking is a dead giveaway that frankly, you don't give damn about golf.

Special thanks to George Peper, Editor-in-Chief, *Golf Magazine,* New York, New York; and Stephen Baker, author of *How to Play Golf in the Low 120's.*

Talking With Gourmet Cooks

When did our taste buds begin to become an endangered species? We consider one who consumes slippery spoonfuls of caviar straight from a chilled can to be the loftiest of gastronomes. But only a Philistine would eat tuna from a tin. We think *boulette de viande* on the menu sounds absolutely divine, but would snub any fine-dining room that dared call it what it is, meatballs.

Obviously, when it comes to matters of cuisine, we're letting prejudice pulverize our taste buds. And the assault is being championed by the growing number of self-avowed amateur gourmet cooks.

But since this chapter tells you how to get along with them, not convince them that some otherwise terribly decent people really do like catsup on their eggs, I offer the following questions.

ICEBREAKERS

Where Do You Like to Shop?
A matter of grave consequence to the gourmet cook. Ask about the availability of *fresh herbs* in his or her market. The gourmet cook is in perennial hot pursuit of a reliable source.

Have You Been to Markets in Other Cities?
The serious epicure knows how to track down the finest ingredients anywhere in the country.

What's Your Favorite Piece of Kitchen Equipment?

You are inviting your new friend to effervesce about some wonderful *bain-marie*, stockpot, or *spaetzle* maker that he or she "just can't live without." (You needn't divulge that your favorites are a can opener and a corkscrew.)

Also ask, "Is there any piece of equipment you use every day?"

What Kind of Knives Do You Have?

Chefs love to talk about their knives. If you hear the names Wusthuf and Henckles, nod approvingly. To all others, give a noncommittal "Hmm."

Where Do You Dine Out When You're Not Cooking?

Gourmet cooks like to dine at restaurants that are, of course, up to their exalted standards. Ask, "Who is the chef?" and add, "Have you ever been tempted to ask for a recipe?" Gastronomes have been known to pilfer globs of sauce and have them lab-analyzed, rather than give in to the gauche temptation.

What Are Some of Your Specialties?

Save the obvious for last. Ask this only after your other queries have proved, beyond a reasonable doubt, that you too are a polished epicure.

Special thanks to Zanne Zakroff, Executive Food Editor and Director of Food Kitchen, *Gourmet* magazine, New York, New York.

Talking With Hairdressers

Hairdressers and barbers are a friendly breed. After all, gossip is their most important by-product.

Equally critical as skill with scissors is their knack for remembering your children's names, the details of your last medical report, and whatever else you have been indiscreet enough to divulge under the influence of perm solution. Blackmail would be a lucrative sideline for them, but at this writing, there has been no such moonlighting recorded.

Making conversation with hairdressers is no problem. They'll do the making. But just for fun, turn the tables.

ICEBREAKERS

Do You Have Your Own Salon? and **Who Are Your Clients?**
These are not indiscreet questions. Tiny salons abound and, unlike cosmetic surgeons, hairdressers relish talking about who their clients are.

Ask, "How many *operators* do you have in your *shop?*" *Shop* and *salon* are interchangeable. Avoid the archaic "beauty parlor."

Does Your Salon Have Other Services, Like Facials, Waxing, or a Nail Technician?
Many salons have these *add-ons* to increase revenue, and the owners boast about their *full-service salons.* And yes, now it's *nail technician,* not "manicurist."

126

Then inquire, "Are the *discount nail salons* cutting into your business?" This is a source of much irritation and lively discussion among the salon-savvy set.

How Many Heads Do You Do Each Day?

HairdresserSpeak for "How busy are you?"

A cautionary note. Avoid the word "beautician." The hip new breed of operator thinks of a beautician as a semiskilled person who does *wash 'n' sets* on the old *blue rinse crowd.* Hmm, makes one think. Almost.

How Would You Describe Your Style? and What Are the Hot New Looks Coming Up?

This question lets the hairdresser feel like the *artiste* he or she dreams of being. If you really want to stroke them, ask "Do you do *consultations?*"

Do You Go to the Hair Shows?

How did you know? Practically all hairdressers go to *hair shows,* which are held throughout the year in most major cities. They are a showcase for new hairstyles and new products.

Be sure to ask, "Have you been to *the International?*" That's the biggie, held in New York every year. She will love telling you what a zoo it's become, how commercial it was, and how all she saw was freaky purple hair and far-out stuff her *clients* (the word "patrons" is passé) wouldn't be caught wearing in their coffins.

When you can take no more, give the hairdresser a final compliment. Say, "You deserve an honorary degree in psychology for keeping your clients happy."

Special thanks to Susan Sommers, Editor, *American Salon,* New York, New York

Talking With Hang Gliders

While your new friend euphorically explains the exhilaration of birdlike flight, you are envisioning bloody crashes into mountainsides and hang gliders breaking in midair.

When the human kite pauses, resist asking the usual stupid questions about safety. Or, if you must, at least preface them by saying "You don't mind if I ask you some *wuffo* questions, do you?" *Wuffos* are people who don't know anything about hang gliding, and they are expected to ask dumb questions. (Stands loosely for "*What for* you want to know that for?")

When this insider's term passes your lips, he'll slap your back and say, "Ask away, buddy. Anything."

Well, almost anything. Do not ask about crashes; hang gliders don't know the word. They call it *going in.* And resist asking, "Don't your arms get tired holding on?" (They're in a harness, you wuffo.)

ICEBREAKERS

What's Your Favorite Launch Method?
Pilots can *cliff launch* or *tow launch.* The first is essentially jumping off a cliff, then getting *lift* from a *thermal*—and hopefully *soaring.* A *tow* or *assisted launch* is with the help of a car or even a plane.

Was Your First Ride Bunny Slope, or Did You Take a Tandem Flight?

Neophyte hang gliders can take off the first time in *bunny slope training*—a solo flight no more than a few feet off the ground. Or they take a *tandem flight*, hooked into a large, two-person glider with the instructor.

What Are Your Preferred Flying Conditions?

Some pilots prefer calm, glassy weather. Others like tail winds or challenging turbulence.

While you are talking favorites, ask about *flying sites* and best seasons.

Have You Ever Done Any Cross-Country?

Some pilots—they like this term better than "hang gliders"—take off and go as far as they can. They optimistically call it *cross-country*.

Ever Done Any Competition Flying?

There are regional, national, and international competitions. The record distance, at this writing, is 303 miles. Pilots are not allowed to fly above eighteen thousand feet.

What Was Your First Flight Like?

The euphoria never wears off. Ask anything about the first flight, and he will glide around the room after you, blithering about the ecstasy, the high, the rush . . .

Special thanks to Jerry Bruning, Executive Director, United States Hang Gliding Association, Colorado Springs, Colorado.

Talking With Horse People

Horse people will tell you they are born, not made. And when, indeed, medical science conducts a study, their contention will be confirmed.

It is positively baffling why some perfectly well-bred city children, the first time they see a horse, run toward the dumb mammal with outstretched arms. Unless they have approached from the rear and it kicks them, these children often enter a one-way door into the horse world.

No other large, four-legged mammal holds the same fascination. One assumes the glamour would rub off on similar animals. Then cow people would speak reverently of cow lovers, cow shows, good cowmanship, and cowback riding. And the stylish cow set would belong to prestigious bovine societies.

But no, the horse alone casts this spell over our young. It convinces them that happiness is hanging around stables, cleaning the mud out of their friends' hooves, sweeping up their manure, and inhaling the odor of their perspiration like a fine perfume.

Who says a horse is a dumb animal?

ICEBREAKERS

Did You Ride as a Youngster?
Many horse lovers were in the saddle before their legs could reach the stirrups. Inexplicably, most of the early addicts are little girls.

Do You Ride English or Western?
Riders usually have a preference. *English* is the saddle in Olympic equestrian events. *Western* has that little cattle-roping horn that you're not supposed to hold on to.

Do You Own Your Horse?
Ask if you think the answer is yes. Usually you can determine by lead-in questions like "Where do you ride?" and "How often do you ride?"

Is Your Horse a Gelding or a Mare?
Horse person's way of asking if the horse is a female or was a male. A *gelding* is a castrated male. Stallions are rarer.
   Ask about the horse's *personality*, not "temperament."

Where Do You Board Your Horse?
If not on her own property, ask about the conditions of the *stable*. How many acres? How many horses? Does it have an *indoor ring*?

Do You Do Much Trail Riding?
Trail riding is pleasure riding through the wilderness.

Do You Show? and What Kind of Showing Do You Do?
These questions are for serious horse people. In *showing*, rider and horse are groomed to the nines. Together they compete in a variety of classes ranging from *walk, trot,* and *canter* up through *jumping* and the precise movements of *dressage*.

What Is It About Horses That Fascinates You?
Sounds like small talk, but obsessive equestrians enjoy sharing their theories, which range from mundane to magical, exotic to erotic.

Special thanks to Mary Kay Kinnish, Managing Editor, and Karen Du Teil, Senior Writer, *Equus* magazine, Gaithersburg, Maryland; and Bill Bohn, Publisher, *America's Equestrian* magazine, Huntington Station, New York.

Talking With Hunters

Are you shocked when the nice man next to you at the dinner party tells you he likes to hunt? Well, if you want to get through the evening with the hostess's crystal intact, avoid discussions of the sport's questionable virtue. The media has made the hunter gun-shy of discussing his sport.

Besides, he'll tell you if God didn't want man to hunt, He wouldn't have given him plaid shirts.

ICEBREAKERS

Do You Hunt Big Game or Small Game?
The logical opener. *Big game* typically is moose, deer, bear, and elk. *Small game* is rabbit, squirrel, and a variety of birds.

Do You Hunt Birds Too?
Good chance he does. Probably *waterfowl* (ducks and geese) and *upland birds* (pheasant and quail).

Hunters just say, "Where do you hunt?" Since particular species are only available in certain places, the answer tells the experienced hunter what his buddy is after.

Do You Hunt With a Dog?
If hunting with a dog is legal in his state, you warm a hunter's heart with this question. Unlike his nonhunting friends and maybe even his wife, his four-legged friend makes no judgments on his sport. Be sure to ask, "What breed do you own?"

132

Have You Done Any Hunting Out West?
Save this for East Coast and Midwest hunters. The premier big game hunting is west of Denver.

Did You Grow Up Hunting?
The best person to learn the sport from was Dad.

Have You Ever Bow-Hunted?
Not as obscure as it sounds. Many gun hunters also enjoy hunting with a bow and arrow or *primitive weapons* (replicas of antique firearms).

What's the Best Hunting Experience You Ever Had?
A must-ask. Stories are the staple of hunter talk.

How Do You Handle the Antis? or **Ever Run Into Any Hunt Protesters?**
Now he'll give you an earful of those "pale-faced little city slicker do-gooders and straphangers who have nothing better to do on a weekend than hassle us."

Do You Fish Too?
More than half of all hunters also fish. If you are squeamish about hunting, switch the conversation to these cold-blooded vertebrates.

Special thanks to Bill Miller, Editor, *North American Hunter,* Minnetonka, Minnesota.

Talking With Insurance People

A wise man told me his surefire method of getting privacy. He tells the talkative person sitting next to him on the plane that he's an insurance salesman. "And then watch 'em clam up," he says.

Pity the poor insurance folk. Most people don't seek their company because their very presence is a reminder that we are a heartbeat away from grisly accidents, horrible diseases, or a home in flames.

Life insurance agents, the public suspects, are the most callous of all. They alone have the pluck to remind us that someday we are going to die. And then, to add insult to injury, they try to separate us from our money while we are still coming to grips with this forbidding thought.

It may come as a happy surprise that many insurance brokers or agents do, in fact, have a heart. Insurance people will appreciate your comprehension of this seldom-recognized fact.

If you should find yourself in the company of an insurance person, the following questions will get your new friend waxing philosophical about his or her industry. Incidentally, if you still suspect he or she is trying to sell you a policy, think of these questions as a tactic to avoid signing on the bottom line.

ICEBREAKERS

What Type of Insurance Do You Deal With? and **Do You Work For a Company or Operate as an Independent Business?**
Obvious openers. Your new friend may work with *property/casualty, health,* or *life*—as an individual or an employee of an insurance company. Or she may be a corporate *risk/insurance manager* who oversees insurance and benefits at her firm.

Do You Consider Yourself an Independent Agent, or Do You Do Business with Primarily One Company? or **Are You an Independent or a Captive Agent?**
Both these questions mean, "Do you represent several insurance companies, or do you sell only one?" Obviously their insider's word, *captive,* could have some negative connotations. Unless you too are an insurance agent, use the first form of the question.

For Life Insurance Agents: **Other Than Selling the Insurance, What Is It that You Do that Makes a Difference For Your Clients?**
Your new friend will want to hug you when you ask this empathetic question. *Selling life* is a very different profession from selling other types of insurance, and it tends to draw a more entrepreneurial type. These folk regret that few people recognize that a good life insurance agent has a mushy side. They like to feel they're designing a product that caring people buy out of love for their families.

Do You Take Advantage of Selling Disability to Your Life Clients?
Increasingly, *life agents* are selling disability and long-term care to their clients.

For Health Insurance Agents: **In The Light of Health Care Reform, How Do You See Your Personal Role Changing?**
Where to begin?

What Do You Think is the Answer to Long-Term Care?
A big problem which is getting bigger every day with our aging population.

For Health and Property/Casualty Agents: **Do You Think the Government Is Getting Too Involved in Regulating the Insurance Industry?**
In a word, yes. But because it's such a passionately debated issue, he or she will enjoy elaborating.

For Property/Casualty Agents: **To What Extent Do You Feel That Claims are Fraudulent?**
A whopping 20 to 25 percent of property claims have some degree of fraudulence.

Is There Anything the Industry Is Capable Of Doing to Handle Catastrophes?
Big issue. Big problem. Ergo, big topic of discussion.

For Property/Casualty Agents with Corporate Clients: **What Role Do You Think Insurance Companies Should Play in Cleaning Up Hazardous Waste?**
As businesses become responsible for pollution and disposing of hazardous wastes, they are looking to insurance for coverage. This gives the corporate property/casualty firm a new challenge.

For Corporate Risk Managers: **With Insurance Becoming so Expensive, What Ways Have You Found to Insure Your Company?** or **Have You Ever Thought of Self-Insuring?**
There is a trend toward large companies providing their own insurance policies.

The flip side of this is asking the insurance agent, "Is the trend toward big companies *self-insuring* affecting your business?"

Are Health Care Reforms Affecting the Employee Benefits Programs that You Buy for Your Companies?
You bet! Ask how.

Special thanks to Jeff Yates, Executive Vice President, Independent Insurance Agents of America, Alexandria, Virginia; Charles Hirsch, Editor, *Life Insurance Selling*, St. Louis, Missouri; Linda Wasserman, Editor-in-Chief, *Risk and Insurance*, Horsham, Pennsylvania; and Evelyn Egan, Managing Editor, *Life and Health Insurance Sales*, Indianapolis, Indiana.

Talking With Kayakers

Over six thousand years ago Eskimos snuggled their muk-luks into the cockpits of kayaks and sealed the reindeer skin around their waists before launching into icy waters.

Today neophyte yuppie *paddlers* jump Reeboks first into their kayaks and feel rugged community with their forefathers. They seal the neoprene-nylon-combo skirt around their Calvin Klein jeans, massage 45 SPF suntan lotion on their faces, fasten their helmets and life jackets, and push out into the heated pool.

After graduating from *paddling school*, the best of them can *run rapids* or contemplate the horizon from the middle of the bay.

Actually, when kayakers reach this point, driving the Eskimo taxi takes some concentration and skill to keep from *eating it* (tipping over). Stifle your desire to ask the routine dumb question, "What happens if you get trapped upside down in the boat?" Lessons will follow on how to satisfy this perverse curiosity.

ICEBREAKERS

What Kind of Paddling Do You Do? or Do You River or Sea Kayak?

Paddling is music to their ears. Say it whenever you can. Kayakers call their passion *paddlesports*. They *go paddling* with *paddling partners* and wear *paddling gear*.

River or *whitewater* kayaks are short and easier to turn while *shooting rapids*. Ocean-loving paddlers prefer the longer *sea kayaks*.

Do You Like to Run the Rapids, or Do You Prefer Flat Water?

This question is for river or whitewater kayakers. Some prefer to race down rivers or run the rapids, and others enjoy maneuvering the kayak into calmer parts of the river where it can *play* back and forth in *holes and standing waves*.

Still other paddlers prefer open ocean waters where they can do battle with the wind and the waves.

Have You Had to Do Many Wet Exits?

A *wet exit* is wiggling out of the kayak upside down and dragging it back to shore, hoping there are no smirking onlookers.

Can You Do an Eskimo Roll?

An *Eskimo roll* is a classic maneuver for when the kayak turns over. The experienced kayaker keeps paddling and flips it back up, seemingly effortlessly, thus avoiding the embarrassing wet exit. Mastering the Eskimo roll or *Eskimo rescue* takes a lot of practice, but most kayakers achieve it sooner or later.

If your new friend is an experienced paddler, adjust your query. Ask, "How long did it take *you* to learn the Eskimo roll?"

Have You Tried Any of the Folding (or Inflatable or Two-person) Kayaks?

Choose any of the above. A purist might scoff at these hybrids, but he or she will enjoy talking about them.

What's the Best Paddling Experience You Ever Had?

Story time.

Special thanks to David Harrison, Editor-in-Chief, *Canoe* magazine, and *Beginner's Guide to Canoeing and Kayaking*, Kirkland, Washington

Talking With Kitists

To jailbirds, flying a kite is passing a clandestine note, cell to cell. To kids, it's instructions to Mom and Dad when told to eat their spinach. But to most of the world, *flying a kite* is either a hobby or a crashing bore.

However, dedicated *kitists* insist it is a sport, an art, or a science—depending on whom you are speaking with.

At kiting competitions, old Asian men flying elaborately hand-painted kites passionately tell Caucasian kids they are missing the point with their aeronautical calculations. The kids tell them painting the kite is a waste of time.

Devotees don't mind, however. They are delighted that kitists come in as many sizes, shapes, colors, and nationalities as the kites themselves.

ICEBREAKERS

Do You Fly a Traditional or Maneuverable Kite? and How Big Is It?

Some *kitists* guide *maneuverable* kites into patterns in the air by manipulating several lines. Others prefer the *traditional* or *nonmaneuverable* one-line kite—just like Charlie Brown's. If a kite spans more than ten feet in width, it is considered big.

How Many Lines Does Your Kite Have?

This a question for the maneuverable kite flier. It probably has two or four lines. A *centipede* kite might have an extra line to guide the tail.

When you ask, "What *kind* of kite is it?" you might hear *box* kite, *parafoil*, or *rokkaku*, which is the traditional six-sided Japanese kite.

Do You Have Trouble Finding Enough Open Space to Fly Your Kite?

This is not kitist small talk. Kite safety and etiquette are important issues to a responsible kitist. It takes a lot of space to fly a maneuverable kite, which swoops around in potentially dangerous loops at about forty to fifty miles per hour. The lines are as strong and as thin as a cheese cutter.

Have You Ever Been Dragged by Your Kite?

A kitist can be *dragged*, not "lifted," by a kite in strong winds. Some enjoy it. They say the art was ruined less than a hundred years ago when they started putting motors on kites, taking the strings off, and calling them airplanes.

Do You Anchor Your Kite, or Do You Hold On to It?

Both large *static* and maneuverable kites can be *anchored* to the ground to prevent dragging.

Do You Fly Your Kite in Competitions?

If yes, ask, "Do you fly as an individual or on a team?"

Do You Do Any Kite Building or Kite Painting?

Many kitists start by purchasing their kites but graduate to creating their own.

Special thanks to David Gomberg, President, American Kitefliers Association, Rockville, Maryland; and Valerie Govig, Publisher and Editor, *Kite Lines*, Randallstown, Maryland.

Talking With Lawyers

Ah, the lawyer. That oft-misunderstood, really terribly decent chap. Case in point. Take old John, the aging millionaire industrialist. His passion was to discover if he could "take it with him." Trusting only three men in his life, he summoned them to his deathbed—his clergyman, his doctor, and his lawyer. He handed each an envelope with fifty thousand dollars and beseeched them to place the envelopes on his lifeless corpse before the lid was closed.

Several days later, at old John's funeral, each of his friends solemnly complied. But seeing old John's coffin being sealed, the clergyman felt a pang of conscience and confessed to his colleagues. "Ah, the hurricane wipeout in Honduras! I had to contribute from John's money. I only put forty thousand in the envelope."

Moved by the confession, the doctor replied, "Yes, Father, regretfully I too had to take from the funds. New equipment at the hospital to save other lives, you know. I only put twenty-five thousand in the envelope."

The lawyer, as you will see, was the most moral of all. "I am shocked at both of you," he exclaimed. "We had an irrevocable fiduciary responsibility to old John. He trusted us. I assure you that in that envelope he has my personal check for the entire amount."

Actually, lawyers can be quite good company—if you know what not to say. Do *not* ask who their clients are. In a social situation, do *not* talk about fees. Do *not* demonstrate massive unawareness of their profession by talking about legal matters which are out of their field. Do *not* tell horror stories about other attorneys.

And never, *never* ask their legal advice on anything. As Abraham Lincoln said, "A lawyer's time and advice are his stock in trade." As others say in a profession similar but older than theirs, "Why give it away free when you can charge for it?"

ICEBREAKERS

Are You a Practicing Attorney?
This question is evidence that you're no legal sloth. Ask this when he or she is simply introduced as "a lawyer." A *lawyer* is anyone who has graduated from law school and *passed the bar*. He or she could be working in any number of fields. A lawyer who is actually *practicing* law is called an *attorney*.

What Kind of Practice Do You Have?
In *private practice* working for herself? With a law firm as an *associate* or a *partner?* Working in government, in industry?

To narrow it down even further, ask "Do you have a *specialty* within your *practice?*"

Do You Ever Get to Court?
Ask if it is not evident from previous conversation. Some attorneys never do any trial work. Others spend their professional lives in the courtroom. You can follow up with, "Do you enjoy *litigation* (or *trial work*)?"

Is Law Becoming Too Much of a Business Instead of a Profession?
Many older attorneys long for the old days when "His Honor" had more to do with honor than with business

Has Our Adversarial System Gone Too Far?

A question for thoughtful attorneys. They must do the best for their clients no matter how obviously guilty they may be. But have we gone beyond the zealous representation that an attorney is supposed to provide? Attorneys have various shadings of opinion on this, depending on the net worth of the accused.

What's Your Opinion of Legal Advertising?

Does the 1977 Supreme Court decision permitting legal advertising serve to better inform the consumer, or has it made the profession look cheap and tawdry?

Do You Like the Kind of Work (Or Cases) You've Been Getting?

A personal question.

Are Lawyers Going to Price Themselves out of Business?

A constant concern. The more humanitarian lawyers actually worry how to reduce costs and improve legal services to the poor.

Who Should Call the Shots in the Rules Governing Attorneys?

The federal government, the states, the American Bar Association? There is conflict in their own ranks on what constitutes "proper conduct for an attorney."

If you are talking with a specialist trained to aid lawyers, called a *legal assistant* or *paralegal*, ask, "Does your firm give you sufficient responsibility?" You're hitting a hot button of a profession which is in a constant state of defining itself. Another whack at the same button is "Do you think that paralegals will ever be able to advise the public on legal matters without the supervision of an attorney?"

Do You Think Law Schools are Turning out Too Many Attorneys?
He will probably nod yes while harboring the superior wisdom that if there are not enough lawsuits to go around, lawyers can always provoke a few more.

What Do You Think is the Future of the Legal Profession?
This invites the attorney to speculate on any aspect he or she wishes, even on how the legal profession is regarded. They know that they're spoken of in the most rancid and unflattering terms and that every chortling writer, at a safe distance, can't resist telling his or her favorite lawyer joke.

And now is the time to get off law and on to his favorite topics, like his yacht or his chalet in the Alps. Be happy that you're having social discourse with a lawyer and are not one of the poor wretches who are forced to pay for it.

Special thanks to Dick Collins, Director of Communications and Public Affairs, American Bar Association; and Gary Hengstler, Editor, *ABA Journal,* Chicago, Illinois.

Talking With Librarians

The bookish spinster balancing spectacles on her nose and a bun on the back of her head is as outdated as the dog-eared catalog cards she kept in old oak drawers. Now we have a cluster of computer programs to confound information retrieval, and a new breed of librarian.

Today's *information professional* graduates from a masters program where he or she learns electronic data processing, systems analysis, mechanized information retrieval, library fund raising, and how to say *shh* with authority.

With all these responsibilities, today's librarian no longer has time to read a book or, heaven help us, suggest a good mystery.

ICEBREAKERS

What Kind of an Institution Do You Work For?
Don't make assumptions that he or she works in a public library or university. Positions can be found in libraries of corporations, hospitals, and large law firms.

What Got You Interested in Librarianship? and **Where Did You Attend Library School?**
The curriculum may be elaborate, but the masters program in *librarianship* is called just plain *library school.*

It is a common misconception that everyone who works in a library is a trained librarian. The tribe checking out

146

books and sneaking a smoke in the stacks may be working at the library just because the hourly rate's better than Dunkin' Donuts.

How Is Your Library Using the New Technology?

An open-ended and volatile question. You may hear about intriguing new uses of computers, or you may induce an attack of convulsions. Some older librarians have severe cases of computerphobia. Others show symptoms of anemia if they cannot get enough technology for their libraries.

Have Funding Cuts Forced You to Curtail Your Services?

Ouch. In addition to curtailing services, dedicated librarians are distressed that they are forced to charge for services that were previously free. It's the *fee or free* headache. They want information to be free and provided equally to everyone.

The more pensive librarians have migraines over the *right-to-know* issue. Who should bear the high costs of the new technology in order to provide information for all—the on-line service, the user, or the library?

Do You Get Involved in the Selection Process?

Be careful of terms. *Acquisition*, in LibrarySpeak, is the routine of ordering the book and checking it in. The *selection process* is actually deciding which books to buy.

Has There Been Any Pressure Concerning Your Selection or the Items in Your Collection?

You are asking about censorship, either internal or from the outside.

Do You Have a Library Cat?

Ask with a twinkle in your eye to show you're kidding. Hundreds of librarians receive mailings from the *Library Cat Soci-*

ety, a no-kidding organization in Moorhead, Minnesota. Their manifesto: "To encourage the establishment of cats in a library environment, and improve the well-being and image of the library cat." Want their newsletter? Ask your librarian to retrieve her latest issue of *The Library Cat* from the wastebasket.

Special thanks to Dr. Peggy Sullivan, Executive Director, American Library Association, Chicago, Illinois.

Talking With Martial Arts Students

There was a time in America when only Bruce Lee movie addicts and Chinatown street gangs knew anything about martial arts. But now the chicken chow mein and sushi crowd flocks to *kung fu* and *karate* schools for fun, fitness, and fighting off muggers. The magnetism and commercialism of martial arts has spread to the younger set. Little kids parade through the malls in their white *gis*, and detergent manufacturers sponsor karate competitions. It's testimony to profound Oriental wisdom (in marketing) that rumor has it a *grand master* must carry a license certifying his fists as lethal weapons.

ICEBREAKERS

What Style Do You Train In?

Always the first question to a martial arts *student*. *Student* is a safe word because even instructors humbly consider themselves students.

The most common are Japanese *karate*, Korean *tae kwon do*, and Chinese *kung fu* and *t'ai chi*.

Confused? Just ask, "What's the *focus* of your *discipline?*"

Whom Do You Train Under?

Even though you probably will not recognize the name (let

alone be able to pronounce it), this is a must-ask. A karate teacher is called *sensei* (sen-say); a kung fu teacher is *Sifu* (see-foo).

Follow up with "What's his background?"

What Prompted You to Start Training?

Physical fitness? Self-defense? Health? Because it's cool, dude?

How Often Do You Train?

Once, twice a week? Also ask, "What's your *belt rank*?" They vary in the different disciplines. In karate, in ascending order, they are: white, yellow, green, purple, brown, and black.

Ask also if he or she competes in *tournaments.*

Do You Train With Weapons? and Do You Go Full Contact or No Contact When Sparring?

In most martial arts training, the movement stops just before impact. If he fights *full contact,* ask, "Do you wear pads when you fight?"

Do You Do Any Other Kinds of Physical Conditioning?

She might say, "No, I just do *forms.*" However, most students run or lift weights to supplement their training.

What Has the Discipline Done for You Psychologically (or Spiritually)?

Ask the more cerebral types this one. The Asian forms of self-defense emphasize the spiritual aspect.

However, if you're dealing with a karate jock, hone the question to, "Do you feel safer on the streets?" or "How do you think it's helped your killer instincts?"

Special thanks to Marian Castinado, Editor, *Martial Arts Training,* and Jim Coleman, Executive Editor, *Black Belt* magazine, Santa Clarita, California.

Talking With Military Personnel

If you are sitting next to a uniform studded with medals, and you sense the only acceptable conversation is "Yes, sir," "No, sir," "I do not understand, sir," and "No excuse, sir," don't be discouraged. Military men and women are trained to show the same expressionless courage, whether facing a shrimp salad or a firing squad. There is usually a real person under all that chest hardware, trying to relax and crying out for communication.

To find a soft spot between the miniature shields, start slowly. If you know you couldn't tell a lieutenant general from a gunnery sergeant, say, "It's been a while since I spoke to someone in the military." (Maybe never?) "What does that insignia mean?"

This should get his branch and rank out of the way. Then switch to noninvasive queries about his personal life. Stay purposefully light with high-ranking military personnel so your questions won't feed their paranoia that they're threatening the national security. They will find your approach a refreshing change from the bureaucratic and impersonal discourse they face daily.

ICEBREAKERS

What Drew You to the Military Life? or What Drew You to That Branch of the Service?
Some *career military people* are born-again patriots and con-

sider *military service* a calling. Others like to put in their twenty years and then retire young and rich enough to enjoy it. And then there are those who just had to replace Mom and Dad. Uncle Sam was the only relative who said yes.

To find out where he or she is stationed, ask, "Where are you *assigned?*" On the average, military people are reassigned every two or three years.

What's Your *MOS*?
Militaryspeak for *military occupational specialty.*

Were You OCS (Officer Candidate School) or Did You Come Out of the Academy?
The academy is either West Point, Annapolis, the Coast Guard, or the Air Force Academy, depending on whom you are talking to.

To find out if he or she is a *lifer* say, "Are you in for a career?"

Do You Find the Constant Moving Stimulating or Trying?
Especially good question for military personnel with families. Some thrive on it, make friends very fast, and gobble up all the local culture and food they can. Others become insular because, by the time friendships start and they develop a taste for North Carolina barbecue or *baba ghanouj*, it's all over.

Let them take the lead on what they call their kids. Even though it is common MilitarySpeak, it could be insulting if you say *military brat* first.

What's Your Favorite Duty Station So Far?
Story time. Ask also, "Have you done any *overseas tours?*"

How's Congress Been Treating You Lately?
Constantly changing. Ask for an update.

How Has the Drawdown Affected Your Particular Work Specialty?

You've hit a hot button with this question. Everyone in the military will continue to feel the impact of the reduction in troop forces.

Other hot topics? Whatever is in the news concerning their isolated world. If it's not gays or women, there will be another issue that befuddles the most reasonable of military minds.

Special thanks to Tom Philpott, Senior Writer, *Army Times, Navy Times,* and *Air Force Times;* and Hope Daniels, Editor, *Military Lifestyles,* Bethesda, Maryland.

Talking With Models

When the bonny lassie in the bony chassis smiles at you, tosses her tresses, and announces she's a model, nod knowingly and say, "Yes, you have a great *look.*"

These insider's words plant the seeds of suspicion in her gorgeous, ambitious head that you know something about the business and, therefore, are possibly able to help her.

Don't blame the poor girl for being single-minded. She's in a competitive line of work where her self-esteem is in halftone, and she will be faded at twenty-six. Male models last a bit longer, but there are fewer of them and fewer jobs. Give the boys equal ego massage.

ICEBREAKERS

Do You Do Mostly Print or Runway?
If she answers *print,* express admiration. Being a *photographic* or *print model* is very competitive.

If she says *runway,* express admiration. It takes talent to twirl around on a runway.

A third possibility is *showroom.* Express admiration. Ask what her special tricks are for staying cheerful during long hours showing clothes to buyers.

Are You Exclusive or Free-Lance?
You are asking if she is *signed with* one modeling agency and

works exclusively through them, or whether she pursues her own clients. If *exclusive*, ask which agency she's signed with.

Do You Do Much Testing?
This question is for wannabes and newer models. Photographers take *test* shots of models to try out new photographic techniques. Their payment is a *print* of the photograph for their *portfolio* or *book*.

Have You Done Any Editorial?
This one is for established agency models. *Editorial* means the more prestigious fashion shots of models in designer bondage leaping over the Taj Mahal. *Catalog* or *advertising* work is what pays the bills when mother, spouse, or roommate doesn't.

How Many Go-Sees Do You Have in an Average Week?
You have just asked how many appointments she has for potential jobs. If the number of *go-sees* is low, express admiration that she doesn't have to go running around to get work. If the number is high, express admiration that her agency *booker* must really like her.

Do You Someday Plan to Move Into Acting?
Gets him or her speculating on retirement—which is never that far away in modeling.

Do You Have Your Head Shot or Composite With You?
The models' *head shot* is a photo of their face. Most models also have a *composite*, which is all of their best positions and suitable body parts in one flier.

Look at it for a long time. Then say, "Nice commercial shot, but it doesn't capture your tremendous presence." Deep.

Special thanks to Monique Pillard, President, Elite Models, New York, New York.

Talking With Money People

In money matters (and deep down everybody knows that it does), we seek guidance from bankers, stockbrokers, economists, money managers, mutual fund people . . .

We assume they know so much more about money than the rest of us that we are utterly confounded when we discover it slips through their fingers as easily as it does ours.

Yet bankers tell us to give them our money to hold on to when they can't even hold on to their pens without putting little chains on them. And those gentlemen who prefer bonds tell us we can double our money by giving it to *them.*

If you're one of those people who suspect the only way to double your money is to fold it over once and put it in your pocket, heed this advice.

One of the mystiques (myths?) of the money world is that there are people in the know and people out of the know. If you're one of those erudite in-the-know folks, you're also in the know about what to ask.

If you're not, these preliminary questions are gracefully composed to be music to the money person's ego. You'll make your new friend feel like a real in-the-know kind of guy or gal who is talking to a very savvy interrogator.

ICEBREAKERS

Whose Money Do You Handle?

Just about every person in every aspect of the money world

handles *OPM*, other people's money, whether it's institutional accounts or, as they say (to avoid the crass phrase "rich folks"), the money of *high net worth individuals.*

Are You Enthusiastic (Depressed) About the Current Market Outlook?

Sounds quite simple, but even the big boys and girls grind this one to death. Asking stock market types is a compliment because they all have ego invested in their crystal-balling abilities. You will, of course, say "enthusiastic" or "depressed" depending on the bullishness or bearishness of the recent financial pages.

With stock market people, ask if they deal on the *buy* or *sell* side. *Buy side* are people like money managers who take other people's money and invest or buy things with it. *Sell side* are people like analysts at brokerage firms who advise the buy side people what to buy.

Follow up by asking if they are going pretty much in the same direction as everyone else or in the opposite.

For bank execs, a good opener is, "Are you on the *lending* or *deposit* side?" If you are talking with lower-rung employees, ask, "Are you *front office* or *back office?*" *Front office* types, like tellers, deal with the public. *Back office* people, like data processing and record-keeping people, don't.

Do You Think the Federal Reserve Is Being Too Tight With the Money Supply? and Where Do You Think Interest Rates are Going to Go Over the Next Year?

Fundamental questions most appropriate for bankers and money people dealing with fixed income investors. Your asking for an opinion puts your new friend up on a fiscal soapbox that she will enjoy pontificating from.

Be careful not to sound like you are asking for advice on where to put your money, unless you're hinting that your new friend should handle it. That's like meeting a dentist socially and asking him to look at your third left molar. Or worse, asking a lawyer about anything legal when the meter's not running.

What Is the Particular Value That You Bring to (Name of Company)?

You're gracefully flirting with a buzzword with this question. Everybody in the money world likes to think he brings extra *value* to the transactions because of his superior smarts. Ergo a *value-added producer*. (Incidentally, those who are not *value-added* are called *commodity* people, meaning they're cogs in the wheel.)

And yet they all have gurus. A good follow-up is . . .

Who Do You Think Is Worth Listening to?

There is a proliferation of newsletters, economists, analysts, and other assorted financial pundits with loyal followings.

Is Your Background in Economics or Did You Go to Business School? or Did You Go to Business School or Did You Come Up Through the Ranks?

Two ways to inquire about business school without flat-footedly asking if your new friend attended. Many financial wizards are very proud that they didn't have formal training and their magic lies in their own strong, bootstrap-pulling arm.

If you sense you're in the presence of a real maverick, be sure to ask, "What's the most interesting *deal* you ever put together?"

Now you can sit back and listen to a long story.

Special thanks to Jordan Goodman, Wall Street Correspondent, *Money* magazine, New York, New York; and Virginia Stafford, Manager, Public Relations, American Bankers Association, Washington, D.C.

Talking With Motorcycle Bikers

If the young man all dressed in leather is introduced as Pig Iron, Rodent, Blaster, or Hawse, you can presume he's a biker. If you suspect he's allergic to soap and water, place bets on it.

Despite their grungy image, which they flaunt at every opportunity, bikers are a fiercely patriotic lot who embrace traditional values—motherhood, country, apple pie, and acid. He'll brag his ol' lady's a *scooter slut* who dances topless at *biker bashes*, and she's a great mom.

Do they talk much? Not in your language.

Start by mumbling, "*Nice leathers!*" Then, if you stick to his *wheels* and never say the word "crash," you might even become an honorary *righteous brother* or *biker chick.*

ICEBREAKERS

What Kinda Bike You Ride?

The one, the only, the *necessary* opening question. His answer may indicate a whole lifestyle. If his lip curls and he snarls, "A Harley," it can mean he lives for his bike. If he answers with a Japanese or Italian name, he's probably more of a weekend rider.

If he *rides* (never say "drives") a Harley, also called *HOG* for Harley Owners' Group, you must ask, "How old is your bike?" Vintage is real *bad.* (That means good.)

What Kinda Riding You Do?

Also, "Do you *tour*?" (do long-distance riding), and "Do you use it to commute?" "Where have you been on your bike?" "What's the longest trip you've ever taken?" "Have you *customized* your bike?"

Show any sincere curiosity about his beloved bike, and the mute, leather-clad creature will demonstrate uncustomary powers of articulation. Who knows, he might even offer you a little *wind in your face* by taking you for a *putt* or *scoot* on his *toy*.

And if you must talk about crashing, use their euphemisms: *downing*, *dropping*, or *laying down* a bike, or getting a little *road rash*.

You Been to Daytona (or Sturgis)?

Now you're talkin'! *Bike Week* at Daytona, Florida, and the blowout in Sturgis, South Dakota, are the two big yearly *biker bashes*. Everything you've ever dreamed, feared, or lusted after in sex, drugs, and rock 'n'roll happens during Bike Week. Or at least they'll say it did.

What's the Helmet Regulation Here? and Have Many Hassles With Cagers?

Sound like innocent-enough questions, but watch his knuckles turn white. Wearing the hated helmet is regulated state by state.

They also hate *cagers*, motorists who pull purposefully in front of them and then say, "Gee, officer, I didn't see that biker. He pulled out of nowhere."

Been on Any Toy Runs?

Watch his leather start to liquefy at this question. It is a source of great pride to bikers that various bike clubs and organizations sponsor *toy runs*. A *run* is a herd of bikers riding someplace. On a *toy run*, bikers ride to a destination and bring a toy, which they donate to an orphanage or a hospital.

You Ride With a Club?

This question has a skull and crossbones. Be careful. It's not like inquiring about membership in the local tennis club, especially if you see *colors* on the back of his leather jacket.

And if you see a skull and crossbones, *don't ask!* Your new friend is one of the "Hell's Angels," who work hard to foster their reputation of being outlaws who'd just as soon stab you as give you a sincere answer. Ninety-nine percent of bikers have a hate/fear/envy/respect complex about the Hell's Angels, also called the *one percenters* or *outlaws*.

But if he's in all black, you will be permitted to live.

Special thanks to Keith Ball, Editor-in-Chief, *Easyriders*, Agoura Hills, California; and David Snow, Editor-in-Chief, *Iron Horse*, New York, New York.

Talking With Movement Followers

Mankind used to anguish over selling souls to the devil, but not to worry. Apparently mankind can now buy them back.

Hundreds of *New Age* disciplines and various *spiritual* and *metaphysical* groups offer soul for sale in the form of titanium pyramids, crystals, rebirthing, or spiritual diets of tofu and waterlily bulb. (Mastercard and Visa accepted.)

And that's not all. We can also purchase any number of over-the-counter brands of *personal power* and *awareness.* Cerebral salespeople hawk seminars for success to tap our "unlimited"—they promise—*human potential.* "And, yes, we have tapes."

Who are these groups? Some are Eastern in influence. Others are intensely religious. Still others are more focused on *awareness training.*

But it's not just aging hippies who misplaced their souls in the Strawberry Fields of the sixties who are flocking to buy new ones. Some very unmetaphysical, results-oriented institutions like the United States Army and the Central Intelligence Agency have been customers of spiritual balms and human potential elixirs.

Will the Age of Aquarius never stop dawning?

ICEBREAKERS

What Does the Group Believe In?
First, a word of warning. "Cult" is a loaded word. Speak rather of *the group* or *the movement.* Group followers have learned to watch their listeners' reactions. If you want to get to the heart of his or her beliefs, you must make the speaker feel comfortable.

Ask, of course, about the group's leader, but be careful of terms. They are very sensitive about accusations of dictatorial leaders. You might say, "Who is *guiding* the group?" Be aware that some so-called *New Age* people feel very independent. Avoid the group questions with them.

You've Used That Word Several Times. What Exactly Does It Mean?
Each movement and philosophy has its own language and buzzwords that the devotees use liberally. Listen for repeated words and pick up on them. For example, followers of the Krishna Consciousness talk of *Godhead.*

What Was It About (the Group or Ideology) That Drew You?
and **Where Were You in Your Life When You Found (the Group or Ideology)?**
A sympathetic question which gets to the heart of why he or she joined.

What Did It Do for You? and **What Are You Getting Out of It Now?**
The purpose of this question is twofold. You are showing personal interest in him or her and doing the follower a favor. Cults, groups, and some ideologies can be extremely helpful for a short time, but sometimes it is difficult for a follower to move on. This question gets him or her to verbalize the benefits and decide if it is still a positive life force.

Questions for people in the difficult-to-define New Age category:

Was It Environmental or Healing Concerns that Drew You to (Name of Belief)?

Your awareness of these two professed motivations for adhering to New Age–type disciplines will encourage open communication.

What Is Your Daily Practice Like?

People who follow what has been called New Age feel that they are *spiritual people,* but not in a traditionally religious sense. Ask them about the practice of their spirituality, but let them bring up accessories like crystals, pyramids, herbs, incense. It's hackneyed for you to ask about any of these optional ancillaries. Instead, ask, "Have you had any mystical experiences?"

A late-breaking flash: Don't say "New Age," and above all "New Ager," to your new friend. The term is rapidly falling out of fashion even with its adherents.

Special thanks to Peggy Taylor, Editor, *New Age Journal,* Brighton, Massachusetts; and Carol Giambalvo, Cult Information Specialist, Flagler Beach, Florida

Talking With Musicians

If you feel that modern music has made great strides back-wards and classical music is much better than it sounds, don't tell any musicians you meet. Music is their life. Most can't afford much else.

Almost anything you ask a musician is fine, if you use the right language. To rock musicians, a job is a *gig*. They don't write or record songs. It's *material*. If it's good, it's *radical*. If they've got good technique, they've got *great chops*. If they have a recording contract, they've got a *deal*.

Get the drift? No? Well, just follow every sentence with *dude*, and you will do just fine.

ICEBREAKERS

What Instrument Do You Play?
Obvious for openers. Musicians love talking about their instrument. Ask where they got it and, if the name would mean anything to you, who the maker is.

Are You Working on Anything Now?
A musician is always *working on* something. Could be he or she is *shedding* (rehearsing) for the next *gig*, recording some new *material*, or trying to pay the rent.

This inquiry also serves another purpose. *Artists* hate to label their music. ("Well, dude, it's kind of eclectic.") Asking

165

them what they're working on lets them tell you what they want to, no more, no less.

Do You Do Any Studio Work? or Do You Play the Clubs?

If he does *studio work*, ask what kind of gigs he usually gets. If he *plays the clubs*, ask if he *tours*. Or maybe he'll tell you he does mostly *private parties*.

Are You Gigging Now? or Do You Have a Steady Gig?

Don't just ask if he's a full-time musician. Say, rather, "Are you *available* full-time?" Far superior to "Have you been able to give up your day job yet?"

Do You Prefer Playing Live or in the Studio?

If he does both, ask the difference. It will get him playing a less rehearsed instrument, his tongue.

Are You Signed to a Recording Contract?

Ask only if you suspect the answer is yes. It's like asking an actor if he's been on Broadway or a runner if she won the marathon.

If you're obviously talking with a major player, ask how his or her record did by saying, "How did it *chart?*" or "How many *units* did it do?" which is a way of asking how many records or tapes it sold. Maybe it *went gold* or *platinum*.

But if he or she is that big, you shouldn't have to ask.

Do You Think a Recording Artist Can Do Better on a Major Label or an Indie?

Indie is for *independent label*. It's the old relative-size-of-fish-and-puddle dilemma.

What Artists Influenced You When You Were Starting Out?

An excellent question in this very artist-driven field.

Some questions for symphonic, ballet, or orchestral musicians:

Who Is Your Conductor? and **How Is He to Play Under?**
This is *the* question for the symphonic or orchestral musician. Music world wisdom says, "Show me an orchestra that likes its conductor, and I'll show you a lousy conductor."

Who Are the Outstanding Makers of Instruments in Your Field?
Another question that's music to the classically trained ear.

Is Your Management Very Aggressive in Getting Funding for Your Orchestra?
As close as you can come to a business-of-the-business question for the musician. Orchestral funding often comes from several sources, such as grants and philanthropic contributions.

You can also ask how aware the community is of their work—another job management should be working on.

How Long Is Your Season? When Is Your Season? and **Where Do You Play in the Summer?**
Three short questions of importance in the orchestral musician's world.

In What Direction are You Taking Your Music Now?
The ultimate question for rock and classical musicians alike.

Special thanks to Mark Tully Massagli, President, American Federation of Musicians, New York, New York; and Andy Secher, Editor, *Hit Parader* magazine, River Edge, New Jersey

Talking With Needlework Artists

Ah, when she tells you she just adores doing needlework, you lean back in your chair. This will be easy conversing. No panic about politically correct thinking, no enigmatic issues. No gender anxiety. (The guilds report 98 percent of those who wield the wicked needle are women.) Just simple sewing circle talk.

Not so fast. For close kinship with a needlework enthusiast, you must speak of her *art*, not her "craft" or "hobby"— and definitely not her "handiwork." Secondly, you need a dexterous tongue, conversant in *needlepoint, cross-stitch, hardanger, embroidery, appliqué, crewel,* and a stitch of other needlework styles as well.

Or, what the heck, you could let the following crafty queries suffice for all.

ICEBREAKERS

What Type of Needlework Do You Do?
First mission is to determine if she is a *cross-stitch, crewel,* or *hardanger* woman. *Counter cross-stitch* maybe?

Do You Do Original Designs, or Do You Work from Charts?
There are hundreds of shops in most major cities and obscure burgs which sell needlework kits. The sampler *chart*

"God Bless Our Home" still sells like hotcakes. The more caustic needlecraft crowd goes for the "God Bless Our Mortgaged Home" edition.

How Did You Get Started in (Name of Particular Enthusiasm)?

For many women, needlepoint is a cherished hobby handed down by their mothers and their grandmothers before them. For others it's something they do to kill the time rather than their husbands.

Also inquire, "Did you take classes?"

Do You Belong to a Guild?

If you suspect she's needle-addicted, ask about these support groups. There are hundreds of guilds across the country and one national guild. They promote the cultural aspect, sponsor exhibits, give courses, bestow annual awards, have a monthly magazine, and are quite liberal in their membership policy. A full 2 percent of the members are men.

Do You Stitch Mostly for Yourself, or Do You Enter Shows?

At this point she may add that she does needlework primarily for gifts.

Do You Find That Your Friends and Relatives Appreciate Handmade Gifts?

How quickly our loved ones become spoiled.

Do You Have Space at Home to Display All Your Art?

A frightfully common problem.

What Project Are You Working on Now?

She will probably reach into her bag and show you.

Special thanks to Nancy Bowers, President, American Needlepoint Guild, Nashville, Tennessee.

Talking With Newspaper Journalists

The old stereotype of Hildy Johnson, pushy reporter, pad in hand, press card in hat, dies hard. Old-timers envision verbal paparazzi bulldozing past confused officials at mine explosions to document the first cries of brand-new widows and orphans, then wringing the story even tighter to squeeze out the last tear for morning commuters in the *bulldog edition.*

But a fresh breeze has blown across the plains, and the blood of Woodward and Bernstein, Anna Quindlen, Jimmy Breslin, Susan Faludi, Russell Baker, Clarence Page, Maureen Dowd, and many others, pulses through ambitious new journalists' veins.

Today's journalists strive, at least, for coverage with compassion. Some see their roles as investigators, analyzers, and explainers of trends and complicated elements of society.

Are all journalists wise and ethical? Of course not. The bright yellow of some journalism will never fade. The difference is that a yellow journalist will make no mark in today's changing newspaper environment.

ICEBREAKERS

What Do You Do at the Paper? or Are You a Reporter or an Editor?

A *reporter* investigates events or people and writes about

170

them. A *city editor* assigns stories and helps decide what gets into the paper. Other writing jobs are *feature writer, correspondent, editorial writer,* and *columnist.*

What's Your Beat? or Are You General Assignment or Do You Have a Beat?

A question for reporters. You are asking, "Do you have an assigned geographical or topical territory, or can you write about anything?" A *beat reporter* might cover the public school system, the courts, sports, etc.

What Type of Stories Do You Give Priority to?

From the answers, you can calibrate the paper's color from pure white to deep yellow. Ask also about the paper's percentage of *local coverage* versus *national coverage.*

What Are Some of the Big Stories You've Done Lately?

Many journalists become deeply involved in their stories and will enjoy telling you everything they couldn't squeeze into the three-inch story.

If you're talking to an *assigning editor,* one who assigns stories to other writers, ask, "What does an individual or organization have to do to attract your attention?" This wording shows you know they are besieged by special interests, and the answer will give you more insight into the editorial policy of the paper.

Who Owns Your Paper?

Insiders always ask. Some are owned by big chains like Times Mirror, Knight-Ridder, Gannett, Newhouse, or Cox. If it sounds like an independent, you can ask if it is *part of a group?* If you are not sure, ask whether it's a *weekly* or a *daily.*

A good follow-up is "Does *ownership* get involved in what stories make it into print?" This is asking about how much freedom the reporter or editor has in the decision. Many journalists worry that advertising affects editorial choices, or that newspapers appeal to the lowest common denominator with too much emphasis on sensationalism, celebrity coverage, and sex.

How Are You Getting Along with Your Computer? or Have You Been Injured by Your Computer?

The first question is for old-timers. Taking away their old manual typewriters was like wrenching a cub from the mother lioness. The second question invokes another kind of painful experience, the increasingly common *RSI* or *repetitive stress injury*.

Has Your Paper Gone Through Any Redesigns?

Much to talk about here. Perhaps their paper recently started using color or graphics. Ask the new breed about *pagination*, a recent revolution in computer technology for newspapers. Some reporters and editors must now compile the text, the graphics, and the photographs on their computers instead of just *outputting type*. A lot of excitement and a lot of resentment about this one.

Does Your Paper Give the Staff Much Guidance on Ethical Concerns?

Whatever your new friend's hot button is, this question pushes it. Responsible journalists wrestle with a host of ethical quandaries like, What is objectivity? What constitutes good taste, or conflict of interest? What about protecting the privacy of sources or individuals? There are issues of quality versus profit, and making news or reporting it. There may be no answers, but the questions are interesting.

What Do You Think Is the Future of Printed News? or What Do You Think Print Can Do to Keep Broadcast From Taking Over?

People's lack of concentration and their fascination with

sound bites and quick-cutting television worry newspaper people.

If you think this argument of *print* losing out to *broadcast* is old, it is. It started to smolder with the old Movietone newsreels, and it burns brighter every day.

Special thanks to James Cesnik, Editor, *Guild Reporter*, Newspaper Guild, AFL-CIO, Silver Spring, Maryland; Mark Sheehan, Public Affairs Director, National Newspaper Association, Washington, D.C.; and Bud Kliment, the Pulitzer Prize Office of Columbia School of Journalism, New York, New York.

Talking With Nurses

That wonderful country which first put man on the moon is now tripping over a chaotic health care system. And guess who's all tangled up in the bloody red tape? Americans rank a nurse somewhere between a bedpan changer and a health care professional saving lives while the doctor is on the ski slopes. Most nurses have done both.

Nurses shield themselves with their own impossible dialect and maze of indecipherable abbreviations. It gets them through their sometimes heartbreaking day-to-night, night-to-day routine.

These few sympathetic questions with just a hint of their patois is medicine for professional wounds.

ICEBRAKERS

Where Do You Practice?
Nurses, like doctors, *practice.* Difference is, they'll tell you, the nurses get it right.

What's Your Area of Specialty Practice?
The four key words—*area of specialty practice*—are incontestable evidence that you are no total stranger to nursing.

What's Your Patient Load? or **How Many Beds Are in Your Unit?**
These are questions for nurses who work in a hospital or

174

nursing care facility. In NurseSpeak they mean, "How many patients are you responsible for?"

Do You Have a Straight Shift or Do You Work Rotation?
Another question for nurses who work in a large *facility*. Put your top teeth against your lower lip, and practice the word *facility*. Much more in-the-know than "hospital" or "nursing home." *Working rotation* is working different shifts.

Does Your Facility Have Mandatory Overtime?
Some facilities charge the nurse with *patient abandonment* if he or she declines *mandatory overtime*.

Does Your Facility Use Computers for Patient Care Documentation?
This question massages a very sore spot. Many facilities use computers to make sure nurses don't dispense one tablet to a patient without hospital reimbursement. Meanwhile, nurses will tell you, they are suffocating under mountains of paperwork to document their patients' conditions.

What Do You Think About Direct Reimbursement for Nursing Services?
A scorching issue. Many facilities receive insurance reimbursement only for certain technical services rendered by nurses. To continue giving care to a needy patient, many nurses must commit creative documentation.

A very poignant subject to bring up, especially with home care nurses, is *elder abuse*. But only a horror story fan should ask about the cases the nurse has seen.

Special thanks to Florence Huey, Editor, *American Journal of Nursing*, New York, New York

Talking With Pharmacists

What a bewildering and awkward linguistic world we would inhabit if we had to avoid the word "theater" when talking with an actor, "restaurant" with a chef, or "farm" with a farmer. Fortunately, we have only one such edict. Do not, even in hushed tones, utter the word "drugstore" to a pharmacist.

That hideous word evokes the long hours the *community pharmacist* spends serving the public—for which devotion, he'll lament, he don't get no respect. The *D* word also conjures up the exasperation suffered by slow or no-paying insurance companies and a host of other complications.

But let us not dwell on the d——, which henceforth shall be known as the *community pharmacy*. A pharmacist might work in a hospital, a nursing home, or some other health care facility.

While nitpicking, a simple word substitution is guaranteed to win the hearts and minds of pharmacists. Every now and then, refer to him or her as a *practitioner of pharmacy*. And when your tongue starts to form "physician," substitute *prescriber*, the way they do.

Kind of puts the pharmacist on top, doesn't it?

ICEBREAKERS

In What Type of Environment Do You Practice?
Sounds stuffy, but this is widespread formal Pharmacist-Speak for "Where do you work?"

Where Did You Attend Pharmacy School?
They may have a fancy way of asking each other where they work, but they still say *pharmacy school.*

Do You Think the Role of the Community Pharmacy Is Changing?
Pharmacists are a rather dedicated lot, so they'll have some wishful thinking on this one. They would like to play a bigger role in their patients' health than just *dispensing* medications. They feel a compelling part of their job, *counseling patients,* is often overlooked. A concept that's become a lingo is *monitoring patient outcomes.*

How Have the Larger Chains Affected the Face of the Pharmacy?
Your new friend the community pharmacist will no doubt have a heated opinion. Many feel larger chains are too *product-oriented.* Others feel chains offer better value.

Do You Own Your Own Pharmacy? or Would You Like to Own Your Own Pharmacy?
If he or she does, be sure to ask about problems with *third party payers.* It tortures the pharmacist that so many insurance companies reimburse for dispensing only. They do not place a premium or a price on the pharmacists' concern and counseling. Nor on volunteer community health care like drug abuse counseling, diabetes awareness programs, or giving free blood pressure tests. So where's the reward for doing a good job?

Are You Involved in Any Community Health Programs?
If you suspect he or she is, ask. Ah, sweet recognition at last.

Special thanks to Angéle C. D'Angelo, M.S., R.Ph., Executive Editorial Director, *U.S. Pharmacist,* New York, New York; and John Hammond, R.Ph., Director of Practice Affairs, Academy of Pharmacy Practice and Management, Washington, D.C.

Talking With Photographers

You take pictures. I take pictures. Professional photographers *make photographs.* They call them *images* and regard the little flashes of frozen time as their cherished art.

But, you contend, all they do is push a button.

True. But reflect upon the plumber who hits the pipe to stop the leak, and then charges $180.35. When the outraged customer asks for an itemized bill, he complies:

Wear and tear on the hammer, 35¢
Knowing where to hit, $180.

A bargain, considering all the training that goes into knowing where to hit.

A photographer just hits a button.

ICEBREAKERS

What Type of Work Do You Do?
Obviously, photography. But to a photographer, this translates, "What's your specialty?" Maybe it's portrait work, landscapes, fashion, photojournalism, shooting weddings and bar mitzvahs, or even dead bodies (legal forensic). *Fine art photographers* show their work in a gallery, and *paparazzi* stalk movie stars and royalty to catch them in compromising positions.

Are You Free-lance or With a Publication?
He or she might be on the payroll of one publication or might grovel before various magazine and newspaper editors to get *assignments.*

Do You Have a Rep?
This is a question for free-lance photographers. It means, "Do you have a representative who does your groveling for you?"

What Kind of Equipment Do You Use?
Ask only if you are a cut above the Instamatic set so you can nod knowingly when he starts talking about various lenses.

Do You Do Mostly Outdoor Shooting? or Do You Shoot Mostly With Available Light?
A question for the hobbyist. Lighting, other than by flashcubes, gets complicated.

What's Your Favorite Kind of Shoot? or Have You Shot at Any Interesting Locations?
Just using the word *shoot* as a noun and *location* for "place" shows you're no shutternerd.

And there is a new word in the biz. Yesterday's shutterbug is today's *shooter.*

Do You Work More in Color or Black and White?
Many photographers believe *working in black and white* gives them more leeway for creativity. It is easier to *crop* or *enlarge,* and they can highlight parts of the photograph through *shading.* Most newspapers and some magazines use exclusively black and white. It's also cheaper.

What Do You Do for Processing?
Although some develop their own, most photographers have a favorite *custom lab* that does their color work.

Developing black-and-white photos is a much simpler process. If he works in *B&W*, ask, "Do you do your own *darkroom* work?"

What Effect Do You Think the New Electronic Imaging Is Going to Have on Photography?

A hot subject for photojournalists, art photographers, and many other shooters. New computer imaging and digital cameras are capable of producing high-quality photographic images. This process, called *grabbing an image*, may undercut the photograph's special authority as a record of reality. At the same time, it opens up a new world of artistic possibilities.

Ever Had Any Copyright Hassles?

An especially good question for portrait and wedding photographers. Unless otherwise specified, the photograph belongs to the photographer and cannot be reproduced without his or her permission. Newlyweds and other smiling subjects are constantly violating this stricture.

Are You Putting Together a Portfolio?

Who isn't? All photographers are either putting together a *portfolio* or *book* or adding to their old one. Ask to see it. Even the professional will be heartened by your interest, especially if there's a chance that it might lead to work.

Special thanks to Andrew Foster, Executive Director, Professional Photographers of America; and Vonda Blackburn, Editor-in-Chief, *International Photographer*, Lewisville, North Carolina.

Talking With Police Officers

The best lesson in penology comes from Humphrey Bogart. He taught us, from the big screen, "There are two kinda people in this world, sweetheart. The kind that think cops are the guys that give ya lollipops when you're lost. And them that call 'em pigs."

Assuming you are one of the former, you want to grant the boys and girls in blue their hard-earned respect. And be familiar and friendly.

This is no easy task because police officers have mastered several languages. For example, they talk to the press and their higher-ups about "apprehending the perpetrator." Among themselves, it's "collaring the perp." And those same cops warn the perp that "he's gonna get slammed in the peg."

The following questions include just enough patois to show familiarity with a police officer's day-to-day existence. Not too much, however, lest they suspect that not all of your discourse with them has been agreeable.

ICEBREAKERS

What Agency Are You With?
Just for starters. Short for "What law enforcement agency are you with?" State? Local? Federal?

181

What Do You Do in the Agency?

This question goes for all police officers from the *street cop* to the highest *brass* (CopSpeak for "high official").

A word about *cop*. Cops call cops *cops*. But *you* have to earn that right. Stick with *police officer, trooper,* or *investigator* until you're fast friends. Or until you get a cue from him.

He may tell you he's *general patrol* or has a specialty—called a *detail.*

What's Your Detail? and Are You Plainclothes or Uniform?

These are for the officer *on detail.* For the *patrol* cop, ask . . .

Do You Work Nights?

This isn't just small talk. When the graveyard shift isn't filled with murder and mayhem, it can be a mass of oddball complaints. A far cry from packing lollipops for little lost kids at the mall.

How Do You Feel About Community Policing?

Police departments across the country are trying to bring back the cop on every block who knows the store owners and residents. They feel this neighborhood trust will lead to better security.

How Big an Influence Is Drug Use on Crime in Your Community?

There's not a police officer in the country without a powerful opinion on this one.

What Influence Do You Think Revolving Door Justice Has Had on Your Work?

Cops work hard to *pop* or *collar* a felon, just to see him on the streets again due to overcrowded prisons.

How's Your Boss?

Unless you are talking with top brass, add, "Is he still a cop, or is he a politician?" He'll know exactly what you mean—even if you don't.

Special thanks to Jim Gordon, Editor-in-Chief, *Police Times Magazine*, American Federation of Police, Miami, Florida; and Sara Johnson, Director of Communications, International Association of Chiefs of Police, Arlington, Virginia.

Talking With Private Investigators

There is only one job where being too handsome, too tall, or too charming is a handicap. The private investigator must be a human chameleon and look and talk like Everyman.

If today's successful Everyman wears Gucci shoes and a Burberry trench coat, the PI with successful clients trades in his gum shoes and his seen-better-days trench coat for the same. Instead of the bottle hidden in the desk drawer, he's sipping pure malt whiskey like the rest of the boys in the back of the stretch limo.

All this splendor has gone to some investigators' heads. "Gumshoe," "flatfoot," "shamus," and even "PI" are monikers not worthy of their newly acquired status. They now call themselves, all seven syllables of it, *private investigators.*

Oh, Sam Spade, Mike Hammer, Philip Marlowe, where are you? Don't lament, whodunit addicts. Underneath his eighty-dollar handmade shirt forever beats the heart of a real gumshoe.

ICEBREAKERS

What Do You Concentrate on? or **What Kind of Investigations Do You Do?**
Private investigator's way of saying "What's your specialty?" He may tell you *skip tracing, surveillance, corporate investiga-*

tions or a host of other specialties to uncover people doing what they don't want other people to uncover them doing. ´

Do You Think There Is Too Much Information Available on the Average Citizen?

Probably, but they're glad it's there. Since most are experts on digging through it, they will have a strong opinion on what constitutes invasion of privacy.

Do You Use Any Interesting Equipment in Your Work?

You bet. Their toy boxes and *surveillance trucks* are overflowing with high-tech gear and better spouse traps. How about envelope X-ray spray for reading a subject's mail, a cigarette lighter camera to catch him playing kissy-face at a restaurant, and night vision goggles to catch him ten toes up and ten toes down in total darkness?

Did You Ever Do Police Work?

Especially appropriate for older PIs. Many are retired cops.

Where Do You Get Most of Your Business from? or Where Do You Find (or Advertise for) Your Clients?

Whether he works with the public or for corporations, the PI must seek clients. Who knows, you may be a potential client. Everybody wants to know something about somebody that somebody else doesn't want everybody to know.

Do You Work Regularly for Any Attorneys?

PIs get a lot of business from lawyers and insurance companies who farm out work such as investigating frauds, serving subpoenas, finding missing people, and getting depositions and statements.

Are You Working on Any Cases Now That You Can Talk About?

Be sure to say "that you can talk about." A PI's favorite

phrase is "can't talk about it." He'll use it whenever he doesn't want to answer something or just can't make up his mind.

"Do you want ham on rye or on white?"

"Can't talk about it."

Special thanks to Bob Mackowiak, Publisher and Editor, *PI Magazine,* Toledo, Ohio.

Rapport With Psychiatrists and Psychotherapists

The psychiatrist, that obstetrician of the mind—even at a party we suspect he is analyzing our every response. But chances are he's more interested in strolling back to the canapé table than in crawling up our cerebral intestines.

A psychiatrist is not always looking for undertones in what you say. As Sigmund Freud himself conceded, "Sometimes a cigar is just a cigar."

ICEBREAKERS

What Kind of Practice Do You Have?

This question determines whether he or she is in private practice or works for a hospital, in industry, or in academia. *Psychiatrists* are medical doctors specializing in mental disturbances. The rest of the *psycho* crowd—*psychologists, psychoanalysts, psychotherapists*—are therapists with a variety of initials after their names, but not M.D.

A good follow-up for the hospital psychiatrist or psychologist is, "Do you work with *inpatients* or *outpatients?*"

What Was Your Training? or Do You Have a Particular Orientation?

There was a day when the field of psychiatry was more definable by Freudian, Jungian, Gestalt, Adlerian, and other schools than it is today. But who could expect that the type of man who goes to a topless bar and watches the audience could stay with one traditional doctrine?

Mental health professionals are creating their own hybrids. Now it's more relevant to ask about his or her *training* than *orientation.* "School of thought" is passé.

What Type of Patients Do You Prefer to Work With?
With this question, you are asking to peek into Pandora's box of tragic tales of alcoholics, obsessive compulsives, schizophrenics, coitophobics, bed wetters, and a host of other sufferers of mental disorders.

Where Do You Get Your Patients?
The closest you can comfortably come to a business-of-the-business question. As conversation ripens, ask about *referral networks.*

Do You Have Any Special Techniques for Terminating Therapy?
Propping patients up and pushing them back into the real world is always a challenge for the psychiatrist or psychotherapist.

Is the Way Insurance Companies Are Cutting Costs Affecting the Way You Can Take Care of Patients? or How Badly Have Psychiatrists Been Hit by Managed Health Care?
In a nutshell, pretty bad. But ask, and he'll open up like a patient on the couch. Many mental problems are not reimbursable.

What Do You Think of the Role of Drugs in Psychotherapy?
Psychiatrists can prescribe. Other mental health professionals cannot, but they can have opinions—and do.

What Do You Think of the Proliferation (or Usefulness) of Self-Help Books?
Just for fun.

Special thanks to John Blamphin, Director of Public Affairs, American Psychiatric Association, Washington, D.C.

Talking With Public Relations People

Publicists earn their keep either by throwing the spotlight the client's way and making a big ballyhoo or by keeping the spotlight off after the client makes a big blooper. Whether creating commotion or covering up a client's crimes against nature, the *PR* person's credo is the same: "Thou shalt put no one before Client."

PR people, especially neophytes, are often very attractive and personable. They enter the field because clients will hire them, hoping some of their fresh gloss rubs off on the product. But in time, if the publicists are not careful, some of the product's shoddiness rubs off on them, and young pros grow into old *flacks*.

ICEBREAKERS

Do You Work for an Agency or In-House?
You are asking if he or she works for a *public relations agency*, which can have many clients, or in a particular company's *PR department*.

If the publicist works *in-house*, ask if the company also has an *outside* PR agency working with them.

What Kind of Clients Do You Have? or What Accounts Are You Working On?

This is for agency people. PR types willingly reveal what *accounts* they are working on but might be hesitant to divulge any details of the *campaign.*

What Are You Trying to Achieve for Your Client(s)?
Public relations goals for clients are diverse. For example, *product PR* is not limited to creating goodwill to increase sales. It could involve getting regulatory approval or communicating with shareholders.

Is Your Work More on the Practical Side or the Strategy Side?
Agency folk fall into two main categories, although many work in both. There are publicists who interface with those the campaign is trying to reach, perhaps through the media, and those who conspire with the client on strategy.

Have You Ever Done Any Crisis Preparedness Work for Your Clients?
This is an intriguing side of PR where the agency and the client create a specific program for a corporate crisis situation. Often it's a step-by-step strategy to follow if bad publicity threatens to sink a company.

Do You Work Much With the Media? or Do You Do Special Events?
If she does *product promotion,* ask about *media* involvement and *special events.* Media work is often a matter of *placing* or *pitching* stories through *press releases,* followed by repeated phone calls.

Creating special events can mean dreaming up any extravagant attention-getting device.

Special thanks to Jack O'Dwyer, Publisher and Editor, *O'Dwyer's Newsletter,* and Rosalee A. Roberts, President, Public Relations Society of America, New York, New York.

Talking With (Book) Publishers

People think publishers just print books and sell them. Think again. If Moses were alive today . . .

He finally finds a publisher for the *Ten Commandments.* In the back room the *acquiring editor* is convincing the publicity, sales, art, and production departments.

"Look, the guy's an unknown author, but what the heck. We *took on the title* because he submitted a tight *proposal,* and he swears he's well connected. *Foreign rights* look good, and there's film potential. Heck, *Ten* may not catch on immediately, but it's got great *backlist* possibilities.

"Okay, I'm not suggesting a big *first run.* We could go out and *advance* fifty thousand *units* to the wholesalers, but unless something big breaks at retail, we'd start to see major *returns.*

"Personally, I think we should target the title at the *library market.* No *returns,* no 'gone today, here tomorrow' hassles.

"Hmm, do you think he should shave for the *author tour?*"

Not so simple, right? But the publishing crowd is up to it—an ingenious lot. They have to be. They manage to keep the world's focus on the artistry of their product, while aiming their lens precisely at the bottom line.

Are they talkative?

If they think you are worth talking to

191

ICEBREAKERS

Which Publishing House Do You Work for? and What Department Are You In?

Good opening salvo only if you use the word *house.* Not "company" or "firm" and, above all, not "agency." And do not ask why they call it a house. Nobody knows.

He or she may be in *editorial,* which works with writers in developing the books. Or in *promotions, publicity, sales, rights,* or *production.* The names of most departments at publishing houses are self-explanatory.

Do You Ever Get Involved in the Acquisitions Process?

Starts to get more specific here. You are asking if he or she has any say in which books the house will publish. The role the various departments play in this decision varies from publisher to publisher.

Would You Say that Your House Is More Editorially Driven or Market-Driven?

Only hurl this one when the conversation is going smoothly. You risk sounding like you want to know if he publishes books he really likes or if his first concern is making money. Sales folks, however, are proud of being *market-driven,* that is, choosing a *title* primarily on how well they assume it will sell. Editorial types are traditionally more interested in the subject matter or writing style of the books.

Is Your Company Part of a Larger Company? and Does That Company Have Nonpublishing Activities?

This one is for top management. Publishing houses are becoming part of larger media conglomerates which have profit margins traditionally unreachable by trade publishing. Publishers worry about how to represent diverse cultures, present scholarly works, *give voice* to new writers—and still perform for their stockholders.

How Much Do You Think Technology Is Going to Affect the Book Market?

A big headache. Publishers assume readers won't want to take a novel on CD ROM to the beach. But they fear that typography on printed and bound pages will be a thing of the past for research, reference, and many other works. With young computer geeks replacing *young readers*, publishing management spends sleepless nights worrying about how much to invest in research and development.

Are You Excited About Any Particular Title on Your Current (or Next) List?

On to happier thoughts. This question usually invokes an enthusiastic response. Most people in publishing are interested in the books the house is publishing. Ask if he or she was personally involved with the title.

Note the use of the word *title*. Publishers get tired of saying "book" all day long. They also alternate *list* with *catalog*.

What Drew You to Publishing? and Did You Ever Write?

Good personal questions, especially if your new friend is in editorial. "What type of writing did you do?" and "Do you find any time to do your own writing now?"

What Have Some of Your Bestsellers Been?

This gets them talking about their successes, always a good note to end on.

Special thanks to Michael Coffey, Managing Editor, *Publishers Weekly*, New York, New York.

Talking With Rabbis

Any Jew, or as most non-Jews say, "individual of the, uh, er, Jewish faith," who has graduated from *yeshiva,* a religious school, can be called *rabbi.* It comes as a surprise to the average *goy* (Yiddish slang for "non-Jew") that *rabbi* simply means "teacher."

Becoming a rabbi is an ultimate goal in Judaism. But the rabbi has the classic answer for the priest who, in a moment of ecumenical brotherhood, shares his temporal aspirations.

"You know," confides the priest, "I always dream of becoming a monsignor."

With genetic talent for asking questions, the rabbi says, "And what then, Father?"

"Why, a bishop," the priest answers.

"What then?"

"Well, after that I suppose I could become an archbishop and a then cardinal, Rabbi."

"Humm, what then?"

"Well, then there's only the pope."

"Ahh, what then?"

"Rabbi, there's *nothing* beyond the pope."

"Oh, I don't know." replied the rabbi. "One of our boys made it."

ICEBREAKERS

Are You a Pulpit Rabbi?
When his *yarmulke* or *kipa* (skullcap) nods consent, you may proceed.

What Is Your Affiliation?
You are asking if the congregation is *orthodox, conservative, reformed,* or *reconstructionist.*

Have You Spent Much Time in Israel?
This isn't just like asking Father Jones if he's spent much time in Barbados. Israel is serious stuff. Many Jews feel it is their religious duty to spend time and money in their ancient Biblical homeland.

How Are You Dealing with Assimilation?
A constant quandary. Jews have always struggled to be a part of society and still retain their own tradition and customs. Also ask, "Do you think Jews are becoming more *observant?*"

What Impact Do You Think American Life Has on Judaism?
And vice versa.

What Do You Foresee for Judaism in America?
Probably your last question, since you won't get a word in edgewise once he gets started on this one.

Special thanks to Rabbi Joel Meyers, Executive Vice President, Rabbinical Assembly, New York, New York; and Rabbi Shimon Golding, Director of Marketing, *Jewish Press*, Brooklyn, New York.

Talking With Real Estate People

There was a time when proclaiming "I'm in real estate" gained the listener's immediate respect and envy. How shrewd and foresighted of brokers, investors, and developers to choose a product whose value only goes up. Nowadays, you must squelch your desire to ask what shrewd and foresighted moonlighting they find to ride out the bad times.

With that exception, you need not hedge much else. You will, of course, be tolerant of their slight speech impairment. Real estate people say *rustic* instead of "rundown," *petite* instead of "tiny," *cozy* instead of "cramped," and *secluded* instead of "impossible to find."

ICEBREAKERS

What Aspect of Real Estate Are You Involved in? or **Are You a Broker, Investor, or Developer?**
This uncovers whether he or she sells other people's properties for a commission, invests money in properties, or builds them.

Do You Specialize in Commercial or Residential?
Leaving off the word *properties* gives your question the insider's cachet.

How's the Market in Your Area?

This and the next question are best aimed at brokers. Ask his or her opinion on the direction of interest rates, a matter of extreme concern to anyone in real estate.

What Are Some of the Selling Features of Your Area?

You have read the ingeniously abbreviated ads. "Prime Prof/Resid. Over ½ vcnt. Evict proced in prog. May be del vac. Beautiful prestigious tree-lined street. Surprisingly low taxes. Near airport and shopping."

It's easy to identify *selling features* in ads like these. The good stuff is never abbreviated. The bad stuff is practically indecipherable.

When Do You Think Real Estate Will Become a Popular Investment Again?

Notice that you have optimistically asked *when* and discreetly said *popular,* not "profitable."

What Parts of the Country Do You Think Are Going to Be the Strongest for Real Estate?

Crystal ball time for investors and developers.

Are You Working on Any Deals You Can Talk About Now?

Or ask about his or her most memorable *deal.* Real estate people love to tell war stories, especially the ones they have won.

Special thanks to Mary Fleischmann, Executive Vice President, American Society of Real Estate Counselors, Chicago, Illinois; Frank Clay, Jr., President, National Association of Real Estate Brokers, Washington, D.C.; and Janis Gibson, Managing Editor, *Real Estate Finance Journal,* New York, New York.

Talking With RV Campers

Ah, the birds, the trees, the huge RVs. They're dotting the landscape of rural America—a tribute both to our rugged American pioneer tradition and to our affection for modern conveniences.

A *recreational vehicle* is only one way to go camping, of course. There are tent campers who like to rough it in the wilderness. And spartan backpackers who whittle down the list of necessities to the barest minimum, measuring out inch by inch the amount of dental floss needed for the number of days living primitive.

For these I refer you to the chapter on backpackers. This one, however, is for making congenial conversation with the droves of spunky seniors who are heading for the hills in the comfort of their RVs.

ICEBREAKERS

What Type of Unit Do You Have? and **What's in It?**
Now sit back for a long monologue detailing the RVer's bare necessities for life in the wilderness—the stereo and television, the air conditioning, the carpeting, the microwave . . .

What Facilities Do You Look for at a Campsite?
They might tell you they go rustic or *full hook-up*, which means they hook into the campground's water, electricity, and sewage systems.

Other *facilities* that some RVers insist on are restrooms, organized bingo or euchre games, and ballparks for the kids.

Do You Belong to Any Camping Organizations?
To promote their product, most major manufacturers of RVs have camper organizations which sponsor events. Ask if they go to any of the *rallies.*

Are You a Snowbird?
A question for northern RVers. *Snowbirds* go south in the cold weather.

How Do You Get Around to See the Sights? or What Do You Like to Do When You're Camping?
Visit local attractions on bikes or cycles? Hike? Or like the new tradition of real hot RV grandpas and grandmas, jes' sit around in the wilderness 'n' play with their grandchildren.

Special thanks to DeWayne Johnston, Editor, *Camping Today,* National Campers and Hikers Association, Depew, New York; and Matthew Czoch, Publisher, *RV Trade Digest,* Elkhart, Indiana.

Talking With Rock Climbers

About those walking hardware stores that clank past you during your Sunday stroll in the mountains. From under swinging ropes, hooks, and harnesses, you detect a voicelike sound. It's sputtering to the other two-legged hardware store, "Oh, wow, like it was totally heinous! It was a choss pile—totally gingus. I was way run out over a number 2RP and had to throw for a jizzy sloper. All the while looking at a crater!"

Craters? Could it be Martians beneath the camouflage? Mountain climbers? You're getting close. They call themselves *rock climbers*.

For good rapport with a rock climber, don't make your first question about falling. Rock climbers seldom "fall." They either *come off the rock* (or *wall*), in which case the *belay* rope saves them. Or they *crater* (in which case they're dead.)

These few questions will rescue you from social cratering.

ICEBREAKERS

Where Do You Climb? and **What Type of Climbs Do You Prefer?**
Gets the basics out of the way. You can expect to hear words like *big walls* and *crags*. If you hear numbers like *five-seven* or *five-eight*, your new friend is just talking about grades of difficulty.

Most rock climbing in this country comes under the general heading of *free climbing*. *Free climbers* wear high-friction shoes and climb vertical rock walls using only natural *holds* in the rocks. Their ropes and *protection* set in the rock save them in case they come off the wall.

Aid climbing, which originated in Europe, is climbing by actually using the ropes and gear for moving upwards.

Do You Top Rope or Lead?

This is as close as you want to come to asking, "How good are you?" You are simply inquiring whether he or she is entry-level (a *top roper*) or more experienced (a *lead climber*).

The *lead climber* climbs the rocks first and sets *anchors* that the ropes are attached to. The *top ropers* then climb with the *belay* ropes holding them in case they should *come off* the rock.

Rather than tough mountains or even tough climbs, climbers talk in terms of *pitches*. A *pitch* is the space between a climber's last anchor and the next.

For story hour, ask them to tell you about the *toughest pitch* they ever did, or if they ever got caught in a storm.

Do You Have a Regular Climbing Partner?

Climbers work as partners.

Have You Ever Taken a Long Fall?

By saying *taken a long fall*, you have elevated your query above just asking, "Have you ever fallen?" Climbers feel that sometimes *taking* a fall is part of the total climbing experience.

Did You Have Difficulty Getting Used to the Exposure When You Started Climbing?

This is an open-ended *rock jock's* intellectual question. *Exposure* is preferable to "risk" or "fear."

Have You Ever Been Involved in a Rescue?

He or she might say, "Yeah, like mine."

For You, Personally, Is Climbing More of a Mental or Physical Workout?
Perhaps because rock climbing draws a more cerebral jock, you will hear them talking about the psychological/emotional/intellectual/spiritual aspect of climbing. ("A totally focused mind-body experience, man.") If you get the rock climber going on the mental aspects of the total hardware experience, you're less apt to be subjected to their impossible patois.

Special thanks to Alison Osius, Senior Editor, *Climbing* magazine, Carbondale, Colorado.

Talking With Roller Skaters

What do you do when your market gets too old for your product? You cut the product in half, and sell it back to the same aging consumers at twice the price.

Even Keynesian economists would be skeptical at that one. "Great gimmick," they would concede, "but who could pull it off?"

Well, just when baby boomers looked like they were going to hang up their roller skates once and for all, an enterprising industry took away one row of wheels and doubled the cost.

Now young adults are buying the product at breakneck speed and zipping around on it even faster. The *in-line* skating industry is almost half as large as the ski industry, and revenues are challenging those for tennis.

Will *in-line ankle* soon replace tennis elbow as the hippest sports injury?

ICEBREAKERS

Do You Have In-line or Quad Skates?
How precise of you to say *in-line* instead of "Rollerblade." All *in-line skaters* know Rollerblade is just a trademark, albeit a hot one.

Quad skates are, of course, the traditional four-wheeled ones we rolled around on as kids. Four-wheel purists scoff that in-line is nothing new. They trace the single-line-wheel concept to the rough pavements of the early eighteenth century.

Do You Do Rink or Outdoor Skating? or What Are You Skating on?
Appropriate for both the in-line and quad skater. Quad skaters usually skate in rinks or on pavement. In-line skaters roll along on anything that will hold them—streets, walls, pipes . . .

Have You Ever Been Barred From Skating Any Place?
As more and more in-line skaters buy *speed skates* and zip past cars on major roadways, laws are barring them from certain streets. The *access issue* is becoming a major headache for the industry.

Do You Do Artistic Skating (or Dances)?
These are choreographed movements for performance on skates, either quad or in-line.

Do You Wear Protective Gear?
An obvious demonstration to the in-line skater that you are aware of his courage and the perils he (and the public) face from his skating at such high speeds. The world is waiting for in-line skating to spawn another lucrative market—protective gear for the passing motorist and pedestrian.

For Ice Skaters: **Do You Do Figure or Recreational Skating?**
Quite a few fancy steps beyond *recreational skating* we find *figure skating, speed skating,* and *ice hockey.* If you're talking to one of these fancy gliders, ask also, "Do you compete?"

For Skateboarders: **What Kind of Skating Do You Do?** and **What Are Your Favorite Tricks?**
The first question is not as naive as it sounds. Be prepared to hear about *vert* (skating on ramps), *free style* (on flat land like

a concrete tennis court), or *street.* Even *street* isn't so simple. Skateboarders refer to curbs, poles, even us as *obstacles.*

Tricks? How about the *kick flip* (360-degree turnaround) and *no-handed aerial* (popping off the ground without using hands) or crashing into pedestrians? Great trick.

Special thanks to George Pickard, Executive Director, U.S. Amateur Confederation of Roller Skating Lincoln, Nebraska; Jon Lowden, Editor, *In-Line* magazine, Boulder, Colorado; and Dave Swift, Editor, *Skateboarding* magazine, Oceanside, California.

Talking With Runners

Listen very carefully. Did your new acquaintance at the party say "runs" or "jogs"?

To a runner, a jogger is the weekend would-be jock, shuffling past Sunday strollers with an anguished grimace. He is eternally in agony and constantly gasping for breath.

When talking with *joggers*, keep the questions simple: "Where do you jog?" "How often?" "Do you go jogging year-round?" "Do you jog with a Walkman?"

The *runner*, however, is the real athlete. Just ask him. You will have no difficulty getting him to talk. About his pre-marathon diet (pasta washed down with Gatorade?), his psychology ("Running changed my life!"), and about his minor aches and pains ("But of course I ran through them.")

The following questions keep him going until his healthier-than-thou attitude makes you beg his pardon. "Excuse me while I drag my diseased and frail body back to the bar for another drink."

ICEBREAKERS

How Much Running Do You Do (per Week)?
Runners like to discuss their *training* in *days per week* or *miles per week.*

What Kind of Running Do You Do?
This question invites him to tell you about *hill work, in-*

206

door training, sprints, and preferred running *conditions* (weather).

What Surface Do You Prefer?
Dirt? Asphalt track? Wooden track in the gym?

Do You Do Marathons?
You are asking if he runs competitively, either in locally sponsored races or in larger ones like the annual marathons in New York and Boston. All *marathons* are 26 miles, 385 yards, the exact distance from Windsor Castle to Buckingham Palace. Shorter races, ten-kilometer runs called *10-Ks,* are also very popular.

If he says he runs marathons, inquire which ones. Ask, "Have you ever run *Boston* or *New York?*" Ask about the weather conditions and how many runners were in the race. But *never* ask if he won. That's not the point. And besides, if he had, he would have already told you.

What's Your PR?
When you are feeling comfortable in the conversation, throw this out. *PR* stands for *personal record.* Sometimes they say *PB* or *personal best*—same thing. It means the best time he or she has ever run a particular distance.

Runners love to talk about their personal best. They may even break it down into *splits* for you. *Splits* are their times in sections of marathons.

Have You Ever You Hit the Wall?
Hitting the wall means depleting all the body's resources The runner becomes dehydrated, sweats out all minerals, and his legs lock. Asking is not rude because it happens to all good runners. In fact, he'll be secretly proud that he had the courage and stamina to test the limits of his body.

Runners usually feel very good about their ability to stick with it. A final and fitting compliment is "I really admire the stamina and self-discipline it takes to run." For marathoners, add, "You must feel really tremendous when you've *finished* the marathon."

If a race is coming up, be sure to wish him or her, "Hey, have a personal best!"

Special thanks to Amby Burfoot, Executive Editor, *Runners' World,* Emmaus, Pennsylvania.

Talking With Salesmen and Saleswomen

Don't be bewildered by your new friend's evasive answer when asked the inevitable, "And what do *you* do?" A salesman's customers, friends, and, yea, even his loved ones, suspect he uses unscrupulous techniques to con suckers into buying shabby, overpriced things they don't need.

Why do they think that? Hark, the wisdom we have been weaned on:

"When you stop talking, you've lost your customer."— Estée Lauder

"People will buy anything that's one to a customer."— Sinclair Lewis

"There's a sucker born every minute."— P. T. Barnum

Show your new friend that you're different. Demonstrate your rare insight that he or she really is an artist, a philosopher dealing with weighty concepts like *cold calling, closing the sale, visual aids, telemarketing,* and *list acquisition.*

"Any fool can paint a picture," said Samuel Butler, "but it takes a wise man to be able to sell it."

ICEBREAKERS

Who's the Competition?
A crucial first question after, of course, "What do you sell?"

What's Your Territory? and Where Do You Get Your Prospects?

SaleSpeak for "What area are you responsible for?" and "How do you find your potential customers?"

Do You Work on Commission or Salary?

Salespeople feel comfortable with this question.

Do You Make Sales Calls? and Do You Do Any Cold Calling?

You are asking if he or she actually visits potential or current customers or works mostly by telephone or mail. *Cold calling* is contacting potential customers he doesn't know and who may be unfamiliar with his product or services. Also ask his opinion on the controversial phone sales technique, *telemarketing*.

Is Your Operation Computerized?

Ask what kind of *software* he or she uses to keep track of customers, sales, and *leads*.

Do You Have Any Special Techniques for Closing the Sale? and How Do You Handle Rejection?

Getting the customer to sign on the bottom line is a highly discussed art form.

Concerning rejection, you and I might find it rather unpleasant. But sales pros have seminars on *handling rejection*. Ask them to share some insights.

What's the Toughest Sale You Ever Made?

Story time. Ask about tough *objections* they overcame. Salespeople take expected customer reactions like, "It's too expensive," "Your product's shabby," and "You couldn't pay me to take one of those damned things." They lump them together and call them *objections*. Their philosophy is that *all* objections can be overcome.

Do You Have Any Special Affirmations to Get You Through the Tough Days?

You're showing empathy with the psychological challenges a salesperson faces with this question. Many have phrases they repeat to themselves to keep their spirits up. Others have sales heroes. You could ask, "Who do you think was or is the world's greatest salesperson?" The phrasing of this question echoes a popular modern sales guru with the unlikely first name of "Og."

Sales pros know how crucial a good mental attitude is. Case in point: Two shoe salesmen were sent to a remote island in the Pacific. One cabled back, "Come and get me. They don't wear shoes here."

But the sales pro's hero cabled back, "Send more shoes, no one has any."

What's the Secret of Selling?

Philosophies vary. It could be "knowing your product," "making lots of calls," "never taking no for an answer," or "consistently missing a three-foot putt by two inches." Your question invites the salesperson to take center stage and open a vein.

Special thanks to Og Mandino, author of *The Greatest Salesman in the World, The Twelfth Angel,* etc., and Paul Karasik, author of *Sweet Persuasion.*

Talking With Scientists

My dear, may I introduce you to Harold? You'll so enjoy talking to him. He's a thremmatologist, you know, and his work is absolutely fascinating." And then the hostess disappears leaving you with absolutely fascinating Harold.

Your feeble "Oh, so you're a thremmatologist!" is a transparent bluff which buys you a scant few seconds before it becomes obvious to one and all that you haven't the slightest clue to what a thremmatologist is. You could ask, but you would get the same cursory answer Harold has given hundreds before you.

Take a deep breath and be confident that whether Harold were a nuclear physicist, geophysicist, agrologist, cytogeneticist, eremologist, bryologist, cytologist, orologist, parasitologist, virologist, or any kind of ologist or icist, you would be on safe ground. The following questions will do quite nicely for practically all scientific disciplines.

ICEBREAKERS

What Is Your Field? or What Branch (or Discipline) Are You in?
If the hostess has just introduced Harold as a "scientist," this is your first query.

212

Are You More in the Theoretical or the Applied Side (Discipline)?

Shows you are hip to their esoteric feud. *Theoretical* scientists think of *applied* scientists as nothing more than engineers. The latter return the insult, considering the *theoretical* scientists to be ivory tower fools.

What's Your Specialty Within Your Field?

This inquiry helps head off your having to ask, "Uh, what's that?" The scientist's answer will likely reveal what his or her field is all about.

For example, Harold's *field* of science is thremmatology, and his *specialty* is what he does *within* that field. Harold would have a hard time telling you he is a specialist on indoor propagation cycles without revealing that thremmatology involves the breeding of animals and plants.

What Is Your Current Line of Research?

This gets the ball rolling with a theoretical scientist. If the answer has the ring of hands-on research, you should ask what *experiments* he or she is conducting.

How Is Your Work Funded?

How perceptive, and quite appropriate, of you to ask. He might talk of *big science* projects, which usually involve government funding and many disciplines, or *investigator-initiated* projects funded by the researchers' efforts.

What Direction Is Your Current Research Going in?

Scientists prefer unraveling the mysteries of the universe to making small talk about any less compelling matter. But they will usually reward sincere curiosity because it is such a rare treat.

If you sense that the scientist has *published* on his work—a high honor in the world of science—you may ask, "Has anything *been published* on your work"? Leave it to him proudly to announce, "Why, yes. *I've* published!"

What Do You Think of the Way the Press Covers Your Field?
This question should take you through the rest of the evening. The popular press usually infuriates the scientist who is working in a visible branch of science. In the more obscure disciplines, the professional journals infuriate the scientists.

How Do You Keep Up With New Developments in Your Field?
No matter how obscure his or her field, there are always *new developments*. And it is in a scientist's incurably curious nature to try to keep up with all of them.

Special thanks to Denise Graveline, Director of Communications, American Association for the Advancement of Science, Washington, D.C.; and Marjorie Hect, Managing Editor, *21st Century Science and Technology*, Washington, D.C.

Talking With Scuba Divers

Divers, struggling to stay erect under the weight of their oxygen tanks, regulators, buoyancy compensators, and weight belts, clump past your beach chair to the dive boat.

"Darned fools," you mutter, spreading an extra layer of suntan lotion on your chest.

You lie back to catch some more rays, but several hours later, they rouse you again. This time they are waltzing off the boat, mask and fins in hands, laughing and talking. Their waterlogged bodies seemingly float by, and their eyes are glazed with bloodshot euphoria.

As you're nursing your sunburn, you can't help but wonder what they saw down there—the Holy Ghost himself?

"Close," a scuba diver swears. He or she will tell you the underwater experience is "incredibly peaceful," "like another world," and "the ultimate high."

But like any high, scuba diving becomes addictive. Once hooked, he's not satisfied until he's *dived* Cozumel, Cayman, Cancún. Then he starts lusting after *dive sites* like Truk Lagoon in the Far Pacific, the Great Barrier Reef in Australia, and the Red Sea.

There's lots to talk about with serious scuba divers. You can talk travel: they have been everywhere that has a warm ocean. Talk ecology: they're avid supporters of preservation of undersea life. Talk fish: they know them all. But don't talk seafood.

ICEBREAKERS

Where Have You Dived?
The usual opener, which invites a travelogue of your new friend's favorite diving sites replete with descriptions of the fish, the coral, and the fauna. Ask about the best *site* he or she has ever *dived at.*

It is also perfectly permissible to ask, "How *deep* did you dive?" at any particular dive site, and "What did you see?" Shallow is less than forty feet. Middle is forty to eighty feet, and over eighty is considered deep. The underwater landscapes and types of fish are different at the various depths.

If you hear the diver refer to *the bends,* he is talking about a painful, potentially debilitating or even fatal form of decompression sickness. However, with correct diving, the chance of *getting bent* is slight.

Where (and When) Did You Get Your Certification?
If your new friend has been talking about diving various sites, you can assume he or she is *certified,* a requirement for diving without supervision. *Certification* takes about twenty hours of training followed by an underwater examination called a *certification dive.*

Some diving enthusiasts, called *resort divers,* are not certified. They go to hotels or resorts where, after a few hours of training, they can go underwater with constant supervision.

Do not confuse *scuba* (*self-contained underwater breathing apparatus*) with *skin diving,* which is diving without oxygen tanks, or *snorkeling,* which is swimming close to the surface with a mask and breathing tube.

Do You Prefer Diving on Wrecks or Reefs?
Reefs can provide beautiful landscapes and multicolored fish and coral. *Wrecks* run the gamut from old passenger and warships to sunken airplanes. A diver usually has a preference.

Do You Dive on a Computer?
There has been a recent move toward using a wrist or console computer which lets a diver know how long he or she can stay underwater. Most divers feel it gives them additional *bottom time.*

Are You Into Underwater Photography?
If yes, ask if he or she does *stills* or *video.* Then invite the diver to describe the shots he or she has taken.

Have You Ever Done Any Night Diving?
Some divers think night diving is exciting, mysterious, romantic. Ask about the unusual nocturnal fish and fauna, but don't ask the usual bathtub diver's "You see any sharks down there?" Other divers will complain that they can't see a blessed thing with underwater flashlights.

Special thanks to Fred Garth, Managing Editor, *Scuba Times,* Pensacola, Florida.

Talking With Skiers

Swooping down the *piste,* icy powder blasting his cheeks, the skier forgets the hundreds of dollars of equipment and the days spent, first in planning, then in traveling to the ski town. The cumulative hours in ski lift queues blowing hot air into frozen gloves get lost in the thrill of the *schuss* or the *slalom.*

Skiers are so zealous that they bestow the enviable moniker *ski bum* upon those who have the "courage" to go work for peanuts in a ski town all winter.

ICEBREAKERS

How Much Skiing Do You Get to Do?
This phrasing demonstrates your insight and your sympathy with their plight. No skier ever gets to ski as much as he or she would like to.

What's Your Favorite Ski Resort? and **Where Do You Ski Most Often?**
The full impact of your line of questioning becomes clear only after you have asked both. Only the envied ski bum gets to ski most often in his favorite ski town.

What's the Skiing Like There? or **How Are the Conditions?**
This opens the skier up to talk about the trails or the type of snow—*natural, artificial, powder, icy.* Ski *conditions* of

course change from week to week, day to day, hour to hour, but he or she can generalize about the conditions at various *resorts.*

Do You Prefer Groomed Runs or Do You Like to Ski Off-Piste? and Are You a Bump Skier?

Ways of asking what kind of skiing he or she prefers *Groomed runs* refers to smooth skiing, *off-piste* is off the trail, usually in fresh snow, and *skiing bumps* is going over *moguls* or small bumps.

Have You Been Out West?

A must-ask for all non-Western skiers. Most prefer the powdery snow that blankets the trails in the West. East Coast skiers like to say if you can ski east, you can ski anywhere, because of the icy, hard-packed snow.

Have You Tried Cross-Country or Telemarking?

Although there is not a large crossover, there are two other types of skiing that some *downhill* skiers enjoy.

    Cross-country skis and shoes are lighter, and the skier's heel is unattached for easier traveling over flat territory. *Telemark* skis are a blend of the two and are used in more mountainous regions for climbing up and skiing down in fresh snow.

For Cross-Country Skiers: Do You Do Back Country or Do You Find Groomed Trails?

You are asking whether he or she likes to *break trail* in fresh snow, or go along preprepared snow paths. Ask the cross-country skier where the best *trails* are.

For Telemark Skiers: Do You Enjoy the Ascent or the Descent More?

Telemark skiers first climb up a mountain with skins on their skis and then attempt to ski down in the fresh snow.

Are You Hassled Much by Snowboarders?
The ski purist bristles at the increasing number of noisy kids
skidding down the mountain on their *snowboards.*

Do You Find Any Good Deals on Ski Packages?
A perplexing anomaly. No matter how well-to-do, whenever
skiers get together they always bemoan the price of ski vacations.

Special thanks to Mike Marston, President, American Ski Association,
Englewood, Colorado.

Talking With Skydivers

Predictably, the first question that comes to your rational and inquiring mind is "Why in blazes would you want to jump out of a perfectly good airplane?"

Suspend your curiosity until you have taken a moment to express your admiration for his or her spirit of adventure. Then, as with all thrill sports enthusiasts, your question of "How does it *feel*?" will be enthusiastically addressed.

A parenthetical note here. You would not, of course, be so tasteless as to ask what happens in the unlikely event that neither his parachute nor his reserve *canopy* opens. The answer is gruesomely obvious. Skydivers don't "splat" like their more boisterous bungee-jumping brothers. Skydivers *bounce*. A fatal misnomer.

ICEBREAKERS

How Many Jumps Do You Have?
On-target preamble. Both nervous first-time skydivers (often called *kikis* because sheer terror makes their teeth rattle *ki-ki-ki*) and experienced *jumpmasters* log their *jumps*.

If he or she has a hundred jumps or more, an admiring verbal tribute like ooh or ahh is appropriate. Do not ask experienced divers the cliché questions about fear. They don't think about it, so they claim.

In addition to numbers of jumps, skydivers also measure their euphoric ordeal in *hours* of *free fall*.

221

Where's Your Favorite Drop Zone?

SkydiverSpeak for "Where do you like to skydive?" They call a skydiving school or landing field a *drop zone, DZ* for short. Also ask what types of aircraft they have dived from.

Was Your First Jump Tandem or Static-line?

It's hard even for a jumpmaster to become blasé about his or her first jump. It may have been *tandem*, while attached to a jumpmaster, or alone with a *static cord* opening the canopy automatically. A third training technique is *accelerated free fall (AFF)*, where instructors leap simultaneously and alongside the terrified kiki.

Do You Jump Solo, or Do You Prefer Relative Work?

A matter of taste. Some skydivers prefer plummeting toward the earth at 120 miles an hour to be a very personal solo experience. Others like to share the thrill by jumping *in tandem* (two divers).

When skydivers jump in groups, it's called *relative work* or *free-fall formation flying*. They hold hands and make patterns in the air.

What's the Biggest Free-fall Formation You've Been In?

Skydivers experience awesome comradeship, as all downward-bound travelers share reverence for the absolute sovereignty of the laws of nature. Especially gravity.

Special thanks to Sue Clifton, Editor, *Skydiving* magazine, DeLand, Florida, and Jerry Rouillard, Executive Director, United States Parachute Association, Alexandria, Virginia.

Talking With Squash Players

Squashers, thinly veiling their glee, whine that their colleagues are overpaid, overeducated, and spend far too much time on court than is good for them.

A recent exposé (by *Squash News*, naturally) revealed that 92 percent of squashers are college graduates and 67 percent have graduate degrees.

Their combined soaring intellect, however, does not prevent them from voluntarily crating themselves in a four-walled, blindingly white, windowless chamber.

What do they do in these coatrooms? They work up a big sweat smashing and lobbing a little lickety-split ball which ricochets off the walls at speeds up to one hundred miles an hour. No vegetables, these squashers.

ICEBREAKERS

When Did You Become a Squasher?
Admittedly, the question is partly to demonstrate how easily their moniker, *squasher*, falls off your lips. A word of warning: do not even whisper the name of that bourgeois game racquetball in the presence of a squasher.

A squasher is not born overpaid or overeducated. Nor is he born with a silver squash racquet entangled in his umbilical cord. Most began *lobbing* and *hitting rails* later in life, and will enjoy telling you how they discovered the joys of squash.

Do You Prefer the Hard Ball or the Soft Ball Variety?
You're already in an elite circle by knowing there are two types. In the *hard ball* variety, the ball does not slow down on contact. Also, the court is larger, the size of a luxury coatroom. There continues to be a migration toward the *soft ball* variety—probably because squashers, although few will admit it, are aging with the rest of the population.

How Much Time Do You Spend on Court?
Perhaps it is the higher intellect of the average squash player that gives him or her no patience with the article "the." *On court* is proper SquasherSpeak.

When Do You Think Squash Will Be a Full Medal Sport?
Save this one for dedicated squashers. They find it a source of great consternation that one of the oldest sports in the world still has no official standing in the Pan American or Olympic Games. Note the optimistic *when*.

Do You Play More for the Mental Challenge or for the Physical Exercise?
Now you are making the aerobic heart of a squasher beat even faster. They like to think of their game as *racquet chess.* The strategy of the game is to put the opponent in a difficult position just as in the more lethargic, cerebral board game.

Special thanks to Darwin P. Kingsley III, Executive Director, United States Squash Racquets Association, Bela-Cynwyd, Pennsylvania; and Hazel Jones, Editor, *Squash News,* Hope Valley, Rhode Island

Talking With Stamp Collectors

Becoming a *philatelist* is a four-step process which often starts quite young.

Step one: Fascination with tiny, raggedy-edged pieces of paper begins at about the age when a child first discovers there is something called "foreign countries." These are places to which his mind can travel but his tiny body cannot. So he affixes his imagination to the sticky little papers, and his mind soars around the world.

Step two: He begins hoarding these miniature travel posters.

Step three: Mummy and Daddy proudly tell all their friends about their own little philatelist. (It's impossible to pronounce so it *must* be important.)

Grown-ups he hardly knows start asking him about his "wonderful stamp collection" and bringing him stamps from foreign countries. The initial flame of interest has been fanned by prestige.

Step four: Someone asks him how much his collection is worth. Worth? You mean it's worth money too?

A philatelist is born.

But no matter how advanced his years, or how esteemed his status in the eyes of the world, the stamp collector never becomes blasé about stamps or recovers from his initial fascination. And he still basks in the attention his "wonderful stamp collection" earns him.

Although now he is a bit more discriminating. Not just

any gawker's attention will suffice. It must be someone who is *philatelically* sophisticated—like you, as the following questions prove.

ICEBREAKERS

What Area of Philately Interests You the Most?
Mastering the pronunciation of this tongue-twisting word (phil-*ah*-tuh-lee) merits you, at least, a conscientious answer. Your new friend might tell you he or she is into the increasingly popular *postal history*—collecting stamps on envelopes, called *on-cover*, showing rates, routes, and rare uses.

Do You Specialize in Any Particular Country or Topic?
Topical or *thematic* collections could be stamps with pictures of flowers, elephants, or even stamps related to the history of alcoholic drinks. Countless choices. Topical or thematic collections involve more than one country. Hobbyists like to say *collecting the world* or collecting *worldwide.*

If he or she answers *first day covers,* you're discussing stamps still affixed to envelopes that have been canceled on the first day they were placed on sale.

Do You Collect Used or Mint?
You are asking whether the collection consists of canceled or unused stamps.

Do You Belong to a Stamp Club?
The American Philatelic Society has more than fifty-six thousand members and sponsors many activities. There are many other special-interest stamp clubs across the country.

Do You Like to Exhibit Your Collection?
Millions of Americans just buy *new issues* and stash them away in a box. Serious philatelists who like to exhibit their collections tag these people *accumulators.*

Follow up with "How do you exhibit your collection?" Some people keep an album under the bed and bring it out only for indefatigable friends. Others exhibit their collections on display pages in special glass-covered frames and enter local, national, or international shows

Have You Ever Run Into Any Fakes?

Fakes are genuine stamps with new gum or *reperforation* to change their value. *Forgeries* are imitation stamps designed to defraud collectors or postal authorities.

Anyone purchasing an extremely expensive stamp usually buys it subject to *expertization*. If it is not a forgery, the collector receives a *good* certificate.

Do You Think the World Is Issuing Too Many Stamps?

Let him air his anger that the market is being diluted by overissuing. Ask also, "How do you feel about the overpriced stamps that are issued to appeal to children and new collectors?" Mickey Mouse on a stamp, indeed.

Special thanks to Keith Wagner, Executive Director, American Philatelic Society, State College, Pennsylvania; and Harlan Stone, Director of Education, Philatelic Foundation, New York, New York.

Talking With Surfers

Attention, subway surfers. The word is out from big wave country. Life is a beach, and *stoka-boka*! With the help of Valley Girls and Teenage Mutant Ninja Turtles, SurfSpeak is washing across America.

The drag is, by the time you know any totally awesome word crashes on the East Coast, the *rippers* (surfing showoffs) are riding another *humongous set* (big waves). When a word gets so popular that it is even uttered by the *barneys* (uncool nonsurfers) who have never *gotten barreled* (rode in the curling part of the wave), it threatens the *wave-rider's* exclusionary hipper-than-thou status.

SurfSpeak, a language which traces its ancient classical roots back to the 1960s, is constantly evolving. But even if you don't know the difference between your *goofy foot* (your left) and your *natural* (your right), you can communicate with these *watermen*. The raddest maneuver of all is just say *zup* ("what's up"), and let it him take it from there.

If he says *nuch* ("not much") or *jes' kickin'*, the following questions offer a little inspiration. *Stoka-boka*!

ICEBREAKERS

Where Are the Best Waves?
Translation: "Where do you surf?" The surfer will talk about surfing at a particular *break*, but that's getting into micro-geography.

How Long You Been Riding the Waves? or How Long You Been Surfin'?

Only those brought up in the jiggle of neon bikinis and Malibu pretty boys should attempt to speak their faux language. If you are a tenderfoot urbanite, stick to the second form of this question.

Also ask, "How many times do you go out?"

Are You a Long-Boarder or a Short-Boarder?

The kids will tell you *long boards* are for ancient trentagenarians. They feel the *short boards* are for more progressive surfing. And *body-boarders* are animals. Obviously—they're down on all fours.

Do You Surf Year Round?

Probably does unless he is in Maine or Alaska. Saltwater doesn't freeze until well below 32 degrees.

How Would You Describe Your Surfing?

Is it *power surfing* or *trick surfing?* Maybe it's *radical? Cruisy? Aggressive? Stylish?* The terms won't mean much to more-turf-than-surf types. But it's real rad to hear 'em.

If you sense you are not in the presence of a *philosurfer,* just ask . . .

Who's Your Favorite Surfer?

Doesn't matter that you don't know the stars. Just ask why he likes that surfer. Very revealing, dude.

Are You Into Competition?

He might tell you he's a pro. Or if he's a *soul surfer,* this gives him the opportunity to squeeze his sour grapes and tell you what egomaniacal money-grubbing jerks the pros on the circuit are.

And now it is time to say goodbye. *Latronic, dude.* (Translation: "See you later on, friend.")

Special thanks to Ben Marcus, Senior Editor, *Surfer Magazine,* San Juan Capis, California.

Talking With Swimmers

When someone tells you at the party, "I'm a swimmer," first determine whether you are having a drink with an occasional fanny-dipper or a serious swimmer. Easily accomplished by asking the obvious, "How much swimming do you do?"

If it seems your new friend is so enamored of swimming that only incongruous size is preventing her from executing an immediate half gainer into her cocktail glass, carry on with these questions.

ICEBREAKERS

Where Do You Practice?
You notice, I'm sure, the substitution for the word "swim." *Practice* sounds far more professional and, for some reason, waterlogged lips have difficulty pronouncing the word "swim" repeatedly.

What's Your Best Stroke?
Now you will hear words you haven't thought of since summer camp—*freestyle, backstroke, breaststroke, butterfly.*

Do You Compete?
If yes, ask, "Which *events* do you compete in?"

"Did you compete in college?" is another of the swim set's usual questions. Most did.

Are You on a Team?
Only hitch here is not to say "*swim* team." Same waterlogged labial occlusion.

Do You Prefer Relays or Individual Events?
Arbitrary? Not to swimmers, and most will enjoy telling you about their preference.

Do You Train Long Course or Short Course?
Swimmers train either in the fifty-meter Olympic format or in the twenty-five-yard format, which involves more turns.

Do You Shave for Major Events?
Serious competition swimmers, both men and women, shave their bodies for major events. They prefer the word *event* to "competition."

How Do You Keep Your Goggles From Leaking?
Sounds deceptively like an airhead inquiry, but it's serious business to swimmers. If hearing about eyeball suction and saliva will not ruin your appetite for the hors d'oeuvres, ask away.

Were You a Water Baby?
Most competitive swimmers started when they were small enough to practice butterfly in the family tub.

Special thanks to Charlie Snyder, Communications Coordinator, U.S Swimming, Colorado Springs, Colorado; and Kim Hansen, Editor, *Swim Magazine,* Inglewood, California

Talking With Teachers

After years of translating every thought for half-formed minds—and having life perpetually punctuated by classroom bells—it's quite remarkable that a teacher can emerge as anything more than a tall child.

Some confine their childlike persona to the classroom and emerge as philosophers. They lie awake at night gnawing the bedpost, wondering how an archaic school system can respond to the swift changes in the larger society.

And how their pay scale can permit them to keep living in that society.

ICEBREAKERS

What Grade (or Subject) Do You Teach?
Obligatory first question. If you are talking with a high school teacher, ask "What areas are you *certified* to teach in?"

What's Your Student Population Like?
Full-time adults might find *student population* a bit unwieldy, but teachers say it when they want to know students' race, aptitude, and socioeconomic status.

"What kind of school is it?" is another compulsory question on your curriculum. He or she will tell you if it is suburban, rural, religious, and maybe a bit about the school's philosophy.

Are You a Whole Language Teacher?

A very hot issue. Any elementary school teacher will appreciate this question and probably have a strong opinion. *Whole language* is a style of teaching based on the theory that kids will learn faster about that which interests them.

Do You Team Teach?

Team teaching is several teachers sharing responsibility for a class.

How Much Leeway Do You Have for Choosing the Curriculum for Your Class? Do You Get Much Support from the Parents? Do You Get Much Support from Your Principal for Discipline?

Three evidences of your insight and concern for her professional problems.

How Have Things Changed Concerning What Kids Are Bringing to the Classroom?

You are talking heavy social baggage here. When most teachers got their degrees, it was assumed that every kid came from a "good" background. They had a breakfast under their belt when they entered the classroom, and if there was a discipline problem, the teacher called the parents.

Now many (especially inner-city) teachers deal with hungry, severely abused children, alcoholic or drug-addicted parents, and kids who walk to school through gunfire-pierced neighborhoods.

Ask how he or she thinks schools should tackle these fundamental problems. You will not need to ask another question.

Special thanks to Ronald Wolk, Publisher and Editor, *Teacher Magazine,* Washington, D.C.; and Debra Martorelli, Editor, *Instructor* magazine, New York, New York.

Talking With Television and Radio Personalities

Television and radio personalities are those garrulous folk who bring guests into your bedroom that neither of you would have in your living room. The media is spawning more and more of these celebrated chatters, and every host and hostess's choice garnish for the dinner party table is a media celebrity—a local disc jockey, newscaster, or a talk show personality.

If you should find yourself in the coveted seat next to one of these congenial interrogators, turn the tables and become the cross-examiner. With the help of these questions, you can elicit the inside story of the celebrity's life while the whole table tunes in. Then sit back and watch your social ratings soar.

ICEBREAKERS

How Long Have You Been on the Air?

Be sure to say *on the air* rather than "in the biz" (that's for show business types) or "on the job" (that's for everybody else). Unlike off-the-air types, they do not speak of the "office." *Air personalities* go to the *station* and broadcast out of the *studio*.

Did You Start in This Market?
Insider's way of asking if he started in the area where he is now broadcasting.

Do You Come from a Broadcasting Background or (Name of Specialty)?
Radio and TV folk can come from broadcasting backgrounds or from their on-air specialty, such as business, weather, or sports. Many air personalities have a background in the performing arts.

Who Are Your Viewers (or Listeners)? or Tell Me About Your Demographics.
Use the four-syllable word if it doesn't feel bulky on your tongue. Broadcasters say *demographics* all the time. But then they have trained tongues.

For Talk Show Hosts/Hostesses: **Do You Choose Your Own Topics (or Guests), or Do You Leave That to Your Producer?**
The responsibility for choosing topics and guests varies at the different shows. Also ask talk show personalities if they take *call-ins.* And to cut off profane callers, "Do you have a *bleeper button?*"

"What issues do you most enjoy talking about on the air?" gets them talking personally. But don't pick up the topic of a single show and carry the discussion on. When the show is over, it's over.

For Radio People Only: **What Is the Format of Your Station?** and **How Do You Think the Changes in Technology Are Going to Change Your Job?**
DJs might say their station is *adult contemporary, new country, Top 40,* or many other descriptions of their music. Newscasters and talk show hosts speak of *all news* or *all talk.*

The second question evokes a very hot topic, *digital audio,* broadcasting off satellites. Ask about the consequences of this technology for radio in general and your new friend in particular.

A final business-of-the-business question for radio people is "Do you have much direct contact with your sponsors?" Many do. Some love it. Some hate it.

For Newscasters: **Do You Find Local News or National News Is More Important to Your Listeners?**

This question gets them reflecting on their preferences and those of the community.

News folk usually go out and get some news, but much of it comes over the *wire services*, which are now on computer.

For Disc Jockeys: **Have You Met Many of Your Favorite Groups? Tell Me About Them.**

Most DJs (now called *jocks* in the business) are very into their music. One of the perks of the job is meeting music world heroes.

Do *not* ask the hackneyed question about choosing their own music. That primarily happens at college radio stations.

Do You Ever Do Remote Broadcasts?

Remote is broadcasting done away from the studio at a *location* such as a restaurant, a shopping mall, any place where news is happening or a sponsor is paying. It is more common in radio than in television.

A surefire way for business people to win the hearts and minds of broadcasters is to ask about their station's sales manager and their *rate card*, the list of how much commercials cost on their show.

How Have the Ratings Been?

This question comes with a skull and crossbones. Ask only after you are good friends.

Let's take a break now for a public service spot. 1) Don't

pitch some show idea to a talk show personality in a social setting. 2) Don't get the broadcaster mixed up with some other on-air personality. 3) Don't ask advice about your nephew who is just dying to get into broadcasting.

What Direction Do You Think Television (or Radio) Is Going in? or What's the Future of the Business?
To get him or her musing, or grousing, sympathetically. Satellite, cable, videos, computers, digital audio, channel surfing, virtual reality, and a host of other computer chips off the new block are reshaping the business.

Special thanks to Barry Farber, Vice President, Daynet, talk network; and Carole Nashe, Executive Director, National Association of Radio Talk Show Hosts, Boston, Massachusetts.

Talking With Tennis Players

Certain mysteries of humankind will forever remain unsolved. One of them is why millions of otherwise perfectly responsible men and women who are masters of keeping their eye on the corporate ball are obsessed with whacking a fuzzy little jaundiced one back and forth across a net.

When they are not playing tennis, they are talking tennis. They speak incessantly of *consistency, depth, placement,* and *power.* They orally dissect every muscle of the *stance,* the *grip,* the *windup,* the *toss,* the *follow-through.* They serve up slow-motion replays of every lob and volley of revered idols—McEnroe, Borg, Conners, Navratilova, Graf, Lloyd, and Lendl. For an encore, they speculate on their heroes' mental strategies.

But how do the superstars *really* do it?

Personally I suspect they use techniques like Billie Jean King's. She says, "If you're playing against a friend who has big boobs, bring her to the net and make her hit backhand volleys."

There's great wisdom there. But armed with only this story, you would lose any verbal volley with a tennis fan. So just dropshot these questions and look for an opportunity to get off the court.

ICEBREAKERS

Where Do You Play? Do You Belong to a Club? How Often Do You Play?
Common, civil little openers.

Do You Play in a League?
If yes, you are probably talking with a committed tennis player and can proceed to the next question.

What Level Player Are You?
League players won't mind telling you. It's posted on the clubhouse anyway. *A* players are tournament caliber. *B* players are strong club players. *C* is not so strong, and nobody admits to being a *D* player.

Do You Play Singles or Doubles?
An unfair generalization, perhaps, but older players who find it easier to leap across only half a court prefer doubles. There are *men's doubles, women's doubles,* and the sociable *mixed doubles.*

   The players ask each other whether they are *baseline* or *net* players—better playing from the back of the court or close to the net.

What's Your Best Shot?
Personal question to get your new friend talking about his or her *serve, forehand, backhand, overhead smash*—ad infinitum.

   You could also ask if he or she has a *one-handed* or *two-handed* backhand. Chris Evert and Jimmy Conners made this latter, awkward-looking grip popular.

What Kind of a Racquet Do You Have?
If you are not tired of tennis talk yet, ask. The argument rages on between wide body, oversize, and standard head.

Do You Follow the Open?
That's the *U.S. Open* in America. Then there are the *French Open*, the *Australian Open*, and *Wimbledon*, to name only a few.

Be careful with this question. It can lead you into the crazy world of tennis personalities. It's a player's pet topic, but a dead end for a tennis novice who isn't familiar with the major players and their major foibles.

Are You Ranked? or **Do You Have an USTA Ranking?**
Ask this question only when you know you are talking with a serious player. The *United States Tennis Association* ranks players locally and nationally.

For Tennis Pros: **How Long Did You Play the Satellite Tour?**
If you should find yourself in the illustrious company of a tennis pro, throw this out. The long, hard road to becoming a pro starts with the *satellite tour*, followed by the *challenger*, and finally the *grand prix*. You are hitting a pro's sweet spot when you remind him of the early satellite days.

Special thanks to Page Chrosland, Director of Communications, United States Tennis Association; and Irene Sommers, Editorial Administrator, *Tennis* magazine, Trumbull, Connecticut.

Talking With Travel Agents

Fantasies of rubbing shoulders with the rich and knees with the beautiful has driven many a penniless dreamer to become a travel agent. It is one of the few jobs where they can stay at the same chic resort of the moment, consume the same exotic foods, and massage suntan lotion into their bodies under the same privileged half acre of sun as the abnormally rich.

They are lured by *fam trips*, those freebies provided by hotels and cruise ships to *fam*iliarize travel agents with all their marvels. Everything is gratis for the travel agent except, of course, tips and incidentals.

There's the sticky wicket. To afford even the tips and incidentals, let alone the time off, these would-be jet-setters must stay in the office, ear glued to phone, eyes riveted to computer screen, booking their moneyed clients to the chic resort of the moment.

ICEBREAKERS

Do You Work in a Travel Agency?
Not as naive a question as it sounds. There are many *outside travel agents*, gregarious people who do a lot of networking and never go to an office. Their day is spent at home, making reservations for their pals and funneling them through one or more agencies, splitting the commission.

241

If your new friend is an outside travel agent, he or she will soon ask you who does your travel arrangements.

Is Your Agency an Independent or a Chain?
Smaller agencies feel the threat from *chain* travel agencies, which have superior buying power. Striking terror in the hearts of many mom 'n' pop agencies are very large *mega-agencies* like American Express.

Ask smaller agency owners, "Are you a member of a *buying consortium?*" They are banding together to achieve the clout of their larger competitors.

Is Yours a Full-Service Agency?
The way folks in the *travel and tourism* industry ask about an agency. There are *cruise-only* agencies that make only passenger ship reservations, agencies that book only certain *destinations*, and *full-service* agencies which cover the entire inventory of travel. Travel agents do not make much on just booking airline reservations, so they must increase their services.

Do You Book More Leisure or Corporate Travel?
You have just asked whether she books more travel for business clients or vacationers.

Do You Book Certain Destinations More Than Others?
The key word here is *destination*, not "place." Some travel agents are *destination specialists* and book only one. Others, due to the wishes of their clientele or the size of the commission offered, find themselves booking travel to some destinations more than others.

Do You Make the Itineraries Yourself, or Do You Use a Wholesaler?
If the travel agent books the tours herself, her day is filled with calling airlines and hotels and arranging *transfers*. A

good question for these travel agents is "Do you have trouble collecting from the foreign hotels?" It's hard to dun in a different tongue.

If she uses *wholesalers,* like Thomas Cook or American Express, she books the package for her client, and the supplier takes care of the rest.

Do You Find the Time to Take Many Fam Trips?
Shows you know what this professional perk is all about Then ask where. Travel agents love to flaunt their hardearned freebies.

Special thanks to Eric Freiedheim, Editor-in-Chief, *Travel Agent Magazine,* New York, New York; and Alan Fredericks, Editor-in-Chief, *Travel Weekly,* Secaucus, New Jersey

Talking With Vegetarians

If the person next to you at the dinner party is furtively trying to conceal the roast beef under a lettuce leaf, let the struggle go unnoticed. If, however, your neighbor triumphantly announces to the whole table, "I'm a vegetarian," you're on.

Resist countering with the usual, synchronized with an ingratiating wink at the hostess, "Boy, you don't know what you're missing!"

Do the hostess a greater favor. Get the vegetarian talking with the following questions. The other guests will find the roast more luscious with every answer.

ICEBREAKERS

How Strict a Vegetarian Are You?
The familiar first among vegetarians. Here are possible responses, translated:

Vegan: I consume no foods of animal origin whatsoever.

Lacto-vegetarian: I eat dairy products but no eggs.

Ovo-vegetarian: I also eat eggs.

Lacto-ovo-vegetarian: I consume dairy products and eggs but no animal flesh.

Pesco-vegetarian: I eat fish, dairy products, and eggs.

Semivegetarian: I eat dairy products and eggs, as well as a little fish and chicken, but no red meat.

What Motivated You Toward Vegetarianism? (or a Vegetarian Lifestyle?)

Some people become vegetarians for their own health, others for the health of their chickens, and still others for the health of the environment. And there are those frugal souls who recognize that as their stomachs shrink, their pocketbook fattens.

What Health Benefits Have You Felt Since You Became a Vegetarian?

Invitation to strut his or her stuff.

Do You Try to Buy Only Cruelty-Free Products?

Ask this of vegetarians motivated by humanitarianism. They do not buy leather or other products that involve killing animals.

Do You Try to Eat Organic?

For the environmentally aware vegetarian.

How Long Have You Been Vegetarian?

Vegetarians always ask. Avoid the carnivore's usual naive question, "But how do you get your protein?" The vegetarian is sure to reply that the American diet is excessively high in protein anyway.

Have You Found Any Restaurants that Serve Great Vegetarian Meals?

Dining out is always a challenge, especially for a *strict vegetarian*. Ask also about any special *vegetarian recipes*.

Do You Belong to Any Vegetarian Groups?

In addition to matters concerning their own bellies, various vegetarian groups are active in trying to eliminate world hunger or cruel animal killings in the meat industry. If the vegetarian is involved in the latter, invite him or her to elaborate—*after* the other guests have digested the main course.

Special thanks to Jessica Dubey, Editor, *Vegetarian Gourmet*, Montrose, Pennsylvania; and Lige Weill, President, Vegetarian Awareness Network, Knoxville, Tennessee.

Talking With Veterinarians

A veterinarian invests as much time getting a *D.V.M.* or *M.V.D.* as a physician does getting an M.D. (Your new friend will appreciate being called *doctor,* thank you.) But, unlike physicians, *doctors of veterinary medicine* do not have to put up with hypochondriacs, monstrous medical malpractice suits, or an increasingly suspicious public. But then, neither do they have the advantage of being able to ask their patients what is wrong with them.

ICEBREAKERS

Do You Have a Practice? and What Type of Practice Do You Have?
First and obvious questions.

You might also ask where he or she went to *veterinary school.* At this writing, 60 percent of veterinary students are women. Ask how this might change the face of a currently male-dominated profession.

But it probably will not change the number of syllables they like to hear in their name. Pronounce all six, *vet-er-i-nar-i-an.* Never say "vet."

Do You Have a Special Focus in Your Practice?
You have just invited your new friend to regale you with stories of infestations of microfilaria in the arteries of dogs and

the like. If it is all a tad too technical for you, proceed to the next question.

Do You Work with Companion Animals?

Say *companion animals* instead of "pets like dogs and cats" or "our feathered and furry little friends like birds, hamsters, and gerbils." It merits you a more attentive answer.

"Do you work with *exotics?*" is VetSpeak for asking about birds and reptiles.

If he or she works with larger animals, ask . . .

What Measures Can Be Taken for the Health of Food Animals?

Responsible veterinarians are very concerned about the health and food supply of both farm and wild animals that produce food for humans. Many work with livestock producers on this issue.

Since Your Practice Is So Size and Species Oriented, How Do You Decide on Dosages?

A human doctor's patients are all the same size and species, more or less. But a veterinarian's patients are vastly different. Thus it is difficult to deal within incomplete FDA guidelines of approved drugs and dosages for animals. Computers have been very helpful. The veterinarian punches in the species, size, and weight to help determine dosage.

Is Much of Your Practice Computerized Now?

Veterinarians are very progressive in electronic information and communication.

How Do You Feel About Cosmetic Surgery for Animals?

To conform to breed standards, practices such as *ear cropping* and *tail docking* are common. There are many heated opinions on this practice.

What Do You Think Can Be Done About the Pet Overpopulation Problem?
Throughout the country, more cats and dogs are being born than can be accommodated by responsible owners. Their fate is often incarceration in an animal shelter and eventually death. This issue greatly concerns veterinarians.

Makes one wonder how much sleep physicians are losing over the human overpopulation problem.

Special thanks to Dr. Roland Dommerg, President, American Veterinary Medical Association; Dr. A. J. Kolveit, Editor-in-Chief, *AVMA Journal,* Schaumburg, Illinois; and Dr. Bill Schwartz, American Animal Hospital Association, Denver, Colorado.

Talking With Walkers

Walking? Have they now classified putting one foot in front of the other as a sport? Well, it's considered one by the half-million readers of *Walking* magazine, a publication devoted entirely to burning the shoe leather.

Since walking is an exercise that has no age limitations, increasing numbers of two-legged Americans are taking it up. Senior strollers talk of walking's cardiovascular benefits and are quite happy that it is all gain, no pain.

When one of these sidewalk jocks tells you, "I love to walk," resist the temptation to express your affection for standing. These hoofers are serious.

ICEBREAKERS

Are You a Recreational or Fitness Walker?
A *recreational walker* is not determined to burn up the pavement or set records and enjoys strolling around the neighborhood.

A *fitness* or *exercise walker*, although noncompetitive, is concerned with pace and walks to lose weight, tone muscles, and derive aerobic benefits.

Do You Enjoy the Physical or Psychological Benefits More?
How perceptive of you to be aware of the psychological benefits of walking.

Also ask where he or she likes to walk and what the ter rain is like.

How Often Do You Walk, and How Fast? or Do You Keep Track of Your Pace and Your Distance?

These two are the same question. Save the second version for serious walkers who keep track of their *target heart rate* and their *personal best*, just like runners.

Do You Do Any Race Walking?

Race walking is competitive speed walking. *Race walkers* compete in five-, ten-, or even twenty-kilometer *race walks*. Ask these zealots the same questions you would ask runners, such as, "How do you warm up?" "Do you have any special prerace diet?" "What is the course like?" and "What's your personal best?"

As in all sports, there comes a time when one becomes too old to participate. What's after *Walking?* Are Madison Avenue researchers already contemplating the launch of *Standing*, and eventually *Sitting* magazine? How about *Reclining Today?*

Special thanks to Brad Ketchum, Jr., Chief Editor, *Walking* magazine, Boston, Massachusetts.

Talking With Whitewater Rafters

You wonder what would make anyone with perfectly serviceable arms and legs want to become a piece of human driftwood. Why risk life, and especially limb, thrashing against rocks in whitewater rapids?

Your new friend will tell you one of the big thrills of whitewater rafting is the sound. First, hearing the rush of the approaching rapid. Then the deafening roar when the water's *in yer face*. And finally, the roar behind you after you've come successfully through it. (Oh, you understand—like the thrill when the big Mack truck has narrowly missed your stalled car, and its roar is disappearing down the highway.)

He or she will speak of the tremendous team spirit of "We're all in this boat together." (Soon, "We're all in this hospital together"?) Before deciding your new friend's real motivation is to get his money's worth from his medical insurance, ask the following questions.

ICEBREAKERS

What Rivers Have You Run?
Always the first question, usually prefaced by "Oh, wow . . ."

Do You Go in a Paddle Raft, or an Oar Raft?
Knowing there are two kinds of inflatable whitewater rafts

251

masks any skepticism. *Paddle boats* are the most common for day trips. The larger *oar boats* are used for overnighters when there is more gear to carry.

What Outfitter Do You Go With?

Admittedly, this question does little more than demonstrate your knowledge of the word *outfitter*, a person or company that organizes the rides. You can always follow up by asking, "What do you like about the outfitter?"

What Class Rapids Do You Run?

There are six classes of whitewater rafting. They range from class I, which is a peaceful picnic on water—often called *float and bloat* due to the good food many outfitters provide—to the challenging class VI. Classes V and VI are extremely violent rapids, for experts only. Whitewater rafting is primarily a warm weather sport.

How Many Times Have You Gone for a Swim?

Rafter's jargon for "falling out of the boat." More of that great team spirit—"We're all out of this boat together."

A more serious matter is *hypothermia.* The word has the ring of an unpleasant medical condition and, in fact, means "You freeze, you die."

What Other Rivers Have You Run?

Followed by, "And where else have you been . . . and where else?" Each river run is another badge of honor. The real enthusiasts aren't content until they've run the big ones in Arizona, Colorado, Utah, and Idaho. And the mother of all rivers: "Oh, wow, have you done the Grand Canyon?"

Special thanks to Steve Welch, Manager, American River Touring Association, Groveland, California.

Talking With Wine Connoisseurs

Ah, wine, the drink of the gods, the sweet libation that creates good fellowship among men. Until one of them takes it upon himself to start talking about wine. And, always, it seems, for the sole purpose of mortifying the poor ignorant souls who cannot discriminate between *bouquet* and *aroma.* Not to mention *hollow* and *lean, plump* and *robust.*

If a good *finish* on a wine is having a pie-eyed smile on your face as the last drop rolls down your gullet, this elementary offering is for you.

ICEBREAKERS

Do You Collect?
A connoisseur might begin with "What wines do you prefer?" But unless you will recognize the names—and if you are not content to sit like a mute intellectual puppy at Socrates' feet—start with this question about collecting.

Where Are Most of Your Bottles From?
A safe question because probably you are more familiar with terrestrial geography than the solar system of wine varieties.

Ask also if he or she has a *wine cellar,* which in American cities is probably a temperature-controlled closet in the penthouse, still called a *cellar.*

Do You Have a Favorite Wine Shop? Do You Go to Tastings? Have You Been to Wine Auctions?
More discreet ways to circumvent your ignorance.

Do You Think California Has Caught Up With Europe?
Most wine virtuosos will sing the praises of French wine over California. But there is the occasional soloist who hums a different tune. Chilean, Australian, and South African wines also have proud but small fan clubs.

Have You Been to Bordeaux? or **Have You Visited Napa?**
Depending on his or her previous answer, ask about these French and California wine regions.

I'm Looking for a House Wine. Anything You Could Recommend in a Good Red (or White) Under Twenty Dollars?
The dollar figure can go up or down depending on your wallet and how rarefied the atmosphere of wine erudition you are circulating in.

If you change the subject now, you will have successfully kept your shameful secret—you'd rather have a Coke.

Special thanks to James J. Holsing, Executive Director, Society of Wine Educators, East Longmeadow, Massachusetts.

Talking With Writers

You realize what would happen to Moses if he were alive today. He'd come down from Mount Sinai with the *Ten Commandments* and spend the next five years trying to get them published.

Let's say Moses takes a month to reduce *Ten* (working title) to "Two" (sample chapters). Then he sends this *proposal* to every *literary agent* and *publisher* who has ever touched a religious theme.

Slowly, very slowly, the rejection letters start dribbling back. Moses combs through them, encouraged and elated by any inadvertent compliment implied in the rejection.

Finally, some small Christian press in the Midwest decides to give it a try, and Moses gets a token *advance*.

But it brings only momentary joy. He fights with his young editor who wants to change "Thou shalt not steal" to "Thou shalt not rip off," and "Thou shalt not commit adultery" to "Thou shalt not screw around."

After almost a year of writing and rewriting, the publisher accepts his manuscript (under the more trendy title, *The Ten Big No-No's*), and it *goes to press*.

By *pub date*, his advance is long gone. And he'll be in hock until the first, if any, *royalty* check arrives. So Moses passes the time groaning to his friends that the publisher has miserable distribution and isn't putting enough into publicity.

Such is the life of a writer.

But I've yet to meet one who would trade in his laptop for

a rash-inducing tie or crippling high heels and the constant chalky taste of lipstick.

In fact, someday the Author Police are going to come and bang on every writer's door and say, "Okay, the jig is up. We found you out. You're having too much fun. You'll no longer be permitted to sit all day in your bathrobe and enjoy just thinking and writing."

ICEBREAKERS

Do You Write Fiction or Nonfiction?

The obligatory first question. It's inconceivable to most writers, except to those few who actually do it, that a writer can do both successfully.

What's Your Specialty?

Every nonfiction writer cultivates a specialty to convince editors that he knows more about something than other writers. The specialty can be business, food, computers, travel, relationships, anything.

Whom Do You Write for?

Notice the all-important *whom.* The *whom* can be *book publishers* or *magazines, newspapers,* or the *corporate market.*

A very business-oriented way of asking the same question is, "Who are your *markets?*" If it's magazines, ask, "What *publications* do you write for?" If it's books, ask, "Who's your *publisher?*" Ask a corporate writer what type of clients he has and what kind of writing he does for them.

If your new friend is a poet, avoid these market-oriented questions. The market for poetry is very slim, so it's best to concentrate on your new friend's artistry. But like art, poetry is difficult to describe. Simply say, "I would love to read your poetry sometime." Or if he or she has committed any of the poems to memory, ask to hear one.

Does Your Fiction Fall into Any Particular Genre?

Obviously for the fiction writer. Historical? Romance? True crime?

How Are Your Editors to Work For?

Shows you know that editors are the freedom-loving writer's bosses. Hence a writer (always the starring character in the ongoing melodrama in every writer's head called *My Life*) creates a personae for them. The current editor is seldom just okay. She is either a dream or a bitch, the designation changing hourly.

Do You Belong to Any Writers' Groups?

The loneliness of the profession drives many writers to join fellow writers for bellyaching, getting health insurance, and ferreting out each other's contacts.

Do not, however, ask a best-selling author about his participation in writers' groups. That's like grilling a dignitary on how much time he donates to console the destitute.

Where Do You Do Most of Your Writing?

Now you are showing sensitivity to the writer's need for an isolated bucolic setting to unleash her genius, preferably within sprinting distance to a midtown editor's last-minute lunch invitation.

One last counsel when talking with a writer. Avoid the obvious, "My goodness, where do you get your ideas?" Writers' heads are swarming with them. The trick is taming *one* that a publisher will buy.

Special thanks to Mark Fuerst, President, American Society of Journalists and Authors; and Jonathan Tasini, President, National Writers Union, New York, New York.

Talking With Yoga Practitioners

Undoubtedly you know a little about yoga. You have seen the snapshots of swami squatting in the lotus position, as cool as a cucumber, in the middle of the motorway, with traffic speeding past on all sides.

And you have seen the twelve required movements in the superimposed photograph, the one that looks like a naked man with twenty-four legs and twelve bottoms, just about to be arrested for insulting behavior in a public place.

Although you are quite content with your current repertoire of leg and bottom movements and have no intention of working up, even gradually, to a preliminary lotus in the middle of Main Street, you can still have meaningful dialogue with a yoga practitioner.

If you're at a dinner party, it is suggested that you do not ask your new friend with the impossible Indian moniker if he dental flosses his nasal passages, performs creative belching exercises, and suffers the volcanic enemas you have read about.

Not all yoga practitioners are such zealots. Most are satisfied emulating a lotus, cobra, frog, peacock, fetus, and pretzel in the privacy of their own homes. And they feel clean enough taking normal showers just like you and me.

ICEBREAKERS

Have You Been Practicing for a Very Long Time? and **Do You Practice Every Day?**

People don't "do" yoga, they *practice* yoga. That doesn't mean they're not getting it right. That's just their preferred verb.

And don't call it an "exercise" or "sport." The *practitioners* will tell you, often with a peaceful glaze in their eyes, that the *technology* is over five thousand years old.

Where Have You Studied? or Who Is Your Teacher?

Another subtle difference. Not where have you "taken lessons." Rather, where have you *studied?* And students of yoga *always* ask about the teacher. "Is your teacher an American?" The name is not always a giveaway.

Are You Vegetarian?

Serious practitioners eat no meat.

What Do You Find Are the Biggest Benefits of the Practice?

Yoga practitioners say that yoga is a *tool* for the development of the entire person—physical, mental, emotional, and ultimately spiritual. Most Americans, however, simply practice yoga for fitness or to relieve stress.

Do not ask your new friend if he or she is a *yogi.* The term is used only for those who dedicate their lives to the technology. Even advanced practitioners pride themselves on being eternal *students* of yoga.

What Are Your Favorite Asana? (pronounced ah-san)

If you are not comfortable with the Indian word, just say *postures.* Postures such as the *lotus, plough,* and *cobra* have made it into popular exercise routines.

If you're at a dinner party, it's suggested you don't ask about the highly touted *vatayanasan* or *wind-relieving pose.* And don't tell your new friend that the one that sounds best to you is the *savasan* or *dead body pose*—flat on your back.

Special thanks to Alice Christensen, Executive Director, American Yoga Association, Cleveland Heights, Ohio; and Swami Matchidananda and Vishnu Jayson, Directors, Integral Yoga Center, New York, New York.

Talking With Zen Buddhists

What a practical linguistic device, our alphabet. It is finite, thorough, and has the aura of all-inclusive totality. *Everything* from *A* to *Z.* All animals from *a*rdvarks to *z*ebras. All metals from *a*luminum to *z*inc. All countries from *A*lbania to *Z*aire. And in this book, all interests from *a*ccountant to . . . well, that's where we hit a snag.

Should we talk of Zulu teachers? Well, then why not French and Italian? Then, of course, Spanish, German, Yiddish . . .

Would readers like to enhance their communication skills with Zoroastrians? The chances of meeting one socially greatly diminished after the sixth century A.D.

Zoologists sounded like an excellent choice. But then the president of the New York Zoological Society callously announced he was banning the politically incorrect word "zoo." Henceforth, the elephants will have to memorize the name "Wildlife Conservation Park."

Fortunately we have an alternative, a very viable one at that. A growing number of people (most notably movie stars, media celebrities, and others one envies deep communication with) are joining a very old religion.

Well, it's not really a religion. A philosophy? Hmm, sort of. How about, like yoga, a technology? Not exactly.

Let's call it, as the practitioners do, just plain *Zen.*

ICEBREAKERS

Where Do You Sit? and **Where Is Your Zendo?**
The essence of the Japanese Buddhism, *Zen* is sitting still in contemplation, a form of meditation. There are short *sittings* and *all-day sittings* from early morning through the evening.

People *practice Zen* at home and often go to a *zendo* or temple where they can *sit* to become self-aware. This is called sitting *zazen* (pronounced zah-zen).

Although there is incense, bowing, chanting, and candles in a Zendo, Zen is not a religion. Buddha is not a god, nor is he worshiped.

How Long Have You Been Practicing? or **How Long Have You Been a Student of Zen?**
Zen practitioners call themselves perennial *students* because there is no final level in self-actualization.

You might also ask, "How are you doing in your practice?" This question invites the Zen student to tell you how far he or she has come in the process of self-awareness.

What Led You to Zen?
A personal exploration. One talks of being a *beginner* or a *mature Zen student.*

Although Zen practitioners prides themselves on being totally tolerant, don't put your new friend's patience to the test by asking the usual, "Are you celibate?" "Can you marry?" "Why do you shave your head?" and "Why is Buddha so fat?" The answers are, respectively no, yes, "Only monks and nuns do," and "I dunno."

Have You Been to a Sesshin? When Was Your Last Sesshin? How Was It?
Zen students like to go once a year to a week-long silent retreat called a *sesshin,* pronounced seh-*sheen.*

Do You Have a Dharma (Spiritual Name)? What Is Your Spiritual Name? What Does It Mean?

Mature Zen students find it easier to achieve self-actualization with names like Mokurai ("thundering silence") or Katsuro ("vital path") rather than Susie or Ralph.

Special thanks to Seigan Shikaryo (a.k.a. Ed Glassing), Head Monk, Dai Bosatsu Zendo, Kongo-Ji, Livingston Manor, New York.

If you have any thoughts or comments about this book, or other ideas on good communication, I'd love to hear from you. Write to me at the following address:

Leil Lowndes
P.O. Box 753
Times Square Station
New York, N.Y. 10108

About the Author

A New York City based consultant on advanced communications skills, Leil Lowndes has coached top executives of Fortune 500 companies to express themselves more effectively. She conducts seminars on the art of dynamic conversation and has written for major publications such as *Psychology Today*, *Redbook* and *New Woman*.